The Book
of
Endtime Wine

Christine Beadsworth

First Printing: 2019

ISBN 978-0-359-36344-5

Fresh Oil Releases
41 Tharina Road
Somerset West, South Africa 7130

https://freshoilreleases.wordpress.com/

All photo collages are done by the author.

Just a Little Extra Explanation…

When the Lord laid on my heart the writing of this book, He was very specific in all details including the dimensions, the colors to be used, the style of the cover. As I recorded His instruction, I thought of Moses up the mountain with God, getting extremely specific instruction for all the elements of the tabernacle. No detail was too small because what was being made in the earthly realm was to represent a truth in the heavenly realm. This Book of End-Time Wine is exactly the way it is to depict spiritual truths. It is 22.22cm x 22.22cm, an exact square, like the measurement given for the Holy of Holies. This is because what is contained in this book was heard in that spiritual place; the place where God meets with His friends face to face, above the Mercy Seat, with the wings of the cherubim overshadowing. This is the next station which the true Church is appointed to occupy. We are moving beyond the altar of incense and the furniture of the Holy Place and we are pressing into the glory. The measurements of this book are also a reference to Isaiah 22:22:

Isa 22:22 *And the key of the house of David I will lay on his shoulder, so that he opens, and no one shuts; and he shuts, and no one opens.*

It is time for the key of the House of David to be made available to the end-time-Church. The release of the sound of the end-time wine will be involved with this handover. We are moving from the Church age to the Kingdom age. It involves a change of station and location in the Spirit. Most books published by the Church up to the this point are rectangular. But it is time for change. Most books are black and white. But it's time for full color. It's time for a word that has dimension and weight and eloquence in the spiritual realm.

The picture on the following page is a view of the bottom of my communion cup.

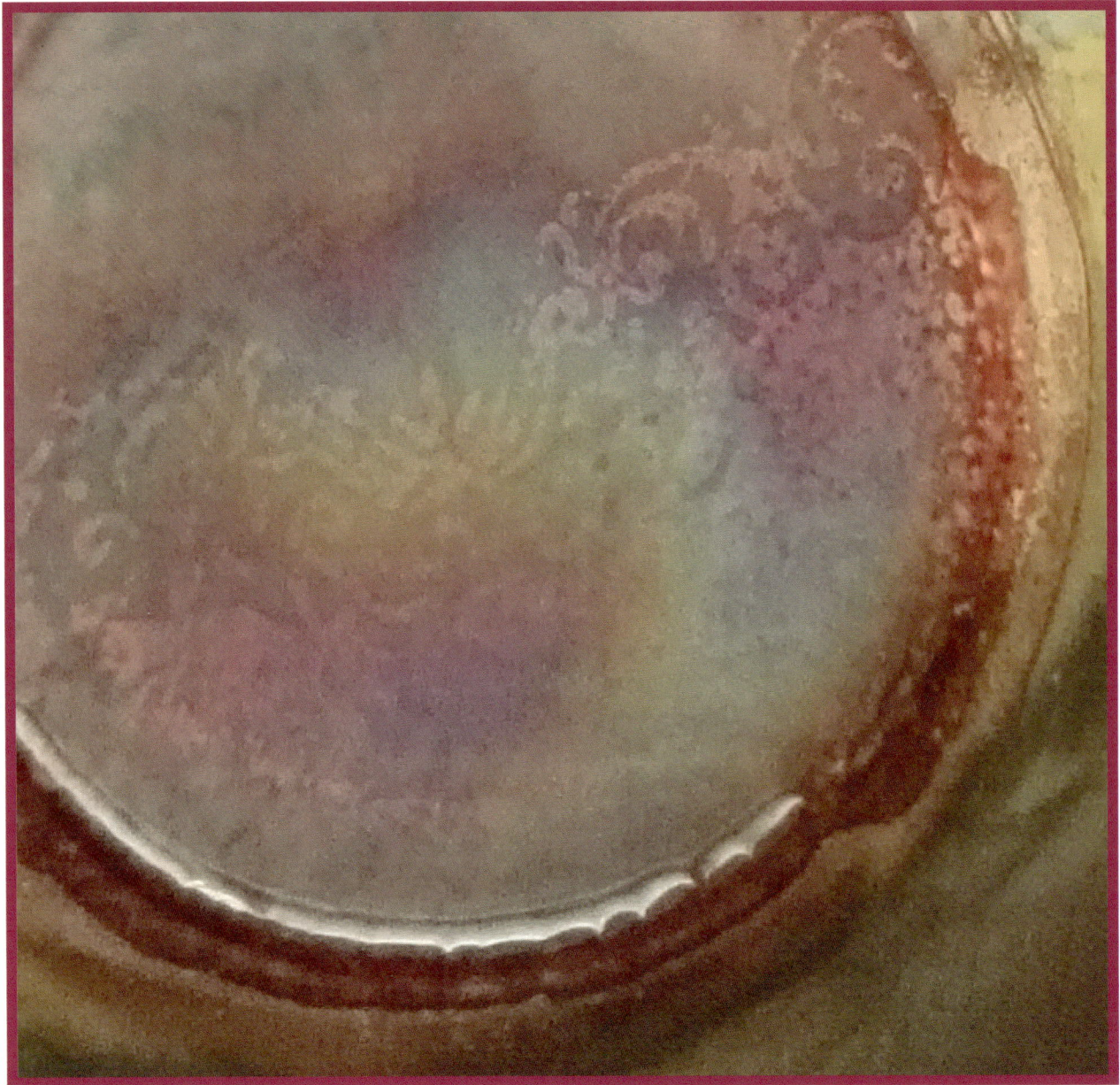

Dedication

To the Master of the Feast,
may You always be filled with joy
as You taste the wine in my earthen vessel,

…and to the Remnant,
who have pressed through the fire
heated seven times hotter,
sustained by their passionate desire
to become a silver vessel,
fit for the Master's use.

Warning and Disclaimer

Contents

Introduction

So what's with the wine? Well, a whole lot actually, especially in these days when the wine in the church has pretty much run out, and Babylon's foul imitation fizzy stuff is being served and touted as the real thing. It's time the water in the stone vessels got turned into wine. But that's a discussion for later…I am notorious for leaping into the deep end before showing my fellow swimmers how to keep afloat. So let me build a foundation for the endtime wine vat to stand upon. Firstly, let me invite you to the feast; to partake of the rich banqueting table provided for me by the Spirit. Let me lay the table and show you what room the banquet is served in. I want you to be fully orientated before I start serving you the cup of Wisdom's spiced wine. Nibble on the bread of the Word as an appetizer and get your bearings.

Wine is about the prophetic fulfillment of the Feast of Tabernacles. Each day during the Feast of Tabernacles, an assistant carrying a silver jug of wine would accompany the High Priest carrying an empty golden jug down to the Pool of Siloam, where the golden vessel was filled with the living water from the Gihon Spring. Then they would return to the temple, accompanied by another group of priests waving palm branches. Then the High Priest and assistant pour out the water and wine simultaneously on the right side of the altar, into a silver bowl which was part of the altar. That is seven outpourings of water and wine during the course of the unfolding feast!

So, on the seventh day, at precisely the time when the priests were pouring out water and wine and circling the altar seven times, Jesus declared that the thirsty must come to Him and drink and this would result in rivers of living water flowing from their innermost beings. Basically, He was saying that before their eyes Tabernacles was being enacted but coming to Him would trigger the manifestation of the spiritual fulfillment of Tabernacles. Continual drinking of the fountain of the water of Life within Christ will result in not only quenching your own thirst but being able to dispense the very same water to others. More than that, the Feast of Tabernacles prophesies an outpouring of wine simultaneously with the water. Does the Book of Joel not speak of a day when God will pour out a double outpouring; both the former and the latter rain in the first month?

The word 'former rain' in Hebrew also means 'teaching, instruction' thereby depicting words from the mouth of God falling like rain. The word for 'latter rain' means 'eloquence'; a flowing of words more like a musical score than a maths lesson. Eloquence is powerful influential speaking; words imbued with an authority that astounds the listeners. We know from Hosea 6:3 that when we press in to know the Lord more intimately, He comes to us as the heavy latter rain.

I believe that the outpouring of water at Tabernacles depicts the former rain and that of the wine signifies the heavy latter rain. Normally former rain falls after the barley seed has been planted in November and the latter rain falls in spring, in order to bring the harvest to full ripeness before Passover. But in Joel 2, they are both being gifted in the first month. Tishrei is the first month of the civil calendar and this is the month when Tabernacles takes place. Significant also is the silver jug which holds the wine and the silver bowl attached to the right side of the altar which receives the double outpouring. Silver speaks of the Word having been purified seven times in a vessel.

On that 7th day of Tabernacles 2018, the spirit opened my eyes to another layer of types and shadows hidden in the actions of the priests. I have the sense they are depicting what will take place during the corporate fulfillment of Tabernacles. During the outpouring on the altar at the prophetic fulfillment of Tabernacles, the assistant carrying the silver jug represents the Bride who has become one with the Lamb; the marriage and consummation or face to face having taken place at Yom Kippur. She is His helpmeet; a priestly silver vessel already carrying water turned to wine within and she accompanies her Bridegroom, the High Priest after the order of Melchizedek, out of the temple and down to the pool of Siloam (meaning 'sent'), which is a storage place for the only source of living water in Jerusalem. He is holding the empty golden jug in His right hand. This vessel represents the manchild; sons of the right hand, which is then filled to the brim with living water. Then they return with the palm branch wavers (who symbolize the coming outpouring of the Spirit) and the water and wine are poured out together, a double portion of outpouring into the silver bowl on the right hand side of the altar and as this outpouring takes place, the meat of the Word is imparted to the silver bowl. The silver bowl is the woman who has been carried to the prepared place in the wilderness and is now being fed with the double portion; water of the Word and wine or meat of the Word.

Of course, the obvious question is, "Where does the wine in the silver jug come from?" It must have been filled before Tabernacles in order to be ready for its part in the outpouring. What is interesting is that the month in which Tabernacles takes place has another name which is not often mentioned. We are told in Kings that Tishrei is also called 'Ethanim', which means 'continually flowing streams', which is odd because in Tishrei, the rain has not yet begun to fall after the winter. So during

Tabernacles, only those rivers which have their source in permanent springs have any water flowing in them.

1Ki 8:2 All the men of Israel assembled themselves before King Solomon at the feast in the seventh month, Ethanim.

The Gihon Spring which feeds the pool of Siloam is such a source. Flowing water is called 'living water' because it is oxygenated. It has the breath of life in it, as opposed to stagnant water, which soon begins to smell. So the golden vessel is filled with living water and the visit to the pool of Siloam depicts coming to Jesus to drink. The silver jug, representing the Bride or helpmeet of the Bridegroom, has already been filled and the water within her has already been transformed to wine. Because she has desired to be a vessel of honor, fit for the Masters use (2 Tim 2:20), her earthen vessel has been transformed to silver, as the Word within her has been refined seven times (psalm 12:6). She is a company of Ethanim, continuous sources of living water and perennial streams, now transformed into wine in the pouring, in order that the guests at the wedding feast may not go thirsty, even though the wine ran out on day 2 of the celebration.

During Tabernacles of 2018 (Tishrei/Ethanim of 5779), the Spirit began to show me some startling revelations about the end-time wine and how He is preparing it. My prayer is that you will take what I share and use it as a guide for prayer, that you too may be a vessel from whose belly flows a river of the best wine.

Chapter 1 ~ The Way to the End-time Wine

I would like to share an experience I had during worship at Tabernacles 2018. As I lifted my hands and began to sing, I heard the Lord say, "Come with Me". He led me down a passageway which seemed to be cut out of rock, going deep down into the depths of the earth. I noticed that all the curved walls were lined with beautiful, semi-precious smooth stones. Finally, we reached a cavern deep underground and He said, "This is my wine cellar and it is here that I store the best wine, kept for the end time". In the centre of the room, I saw a large round wine vat, made of oak. It was open on top and contained glass-smooth ruby colored wine. On the surface of the wine, it looked like there were a few ethereal flames flickering. They were rainbow-colored and I looked closer, wanting to see what they were made of. I realized that they were actually small breezes of seven-fold light which were gently stroking the surface of the wine. "This is where the zephyrs work," the Lord continued, "They are waking the sleeping wine, in preparation for it being poured forth".

I began to sing a new song calling for the wine to be brought to the surface and poured forth and this caused the zephyr breezes to flicker violently, so that it looked as if the whole surface of the wine was on fire. "This cellar is within you," the Spirit whispered and I understood that the journey going deep down was actually accessing the depths within, rather than without, or out in space somewhere. Somewhere deep within was endtime wine waiting to be brought to the surface.

Shortly after this, I was shown an ink bottle and saw a pen being dipped into its contents. The pen then began to write on a blank page and I noticed the ink was a dark reddish purple and sparkled with life. I realized the ink was actually the wine which I had seen in the vat, which the Lord had indicated was reserved for the end time. Then the Lord said quietly, "This is My birthing chamber" and suddenly, the surface of the wine was sucked up like a vortex high in the air above the vat. I could see the wine had substance, dimension and structure and was unlike a liquid. Within its folds, I could see a DNA spiral and it looked like the nucleotide pairs were shelves lined with books. Then the wine subsided again into the vat and I realized He is showing me that within the wine, there are books stored, waiting to be written or birthed. Then I saw many books flying out of the vat and up the beautiful stone-studded passageway towards the light, where I knew people would see them and read their contents and be changed.

I asked the Lord what the significance of the smooth stones lining the passageway was and He replied, "These are the individual jewels discovered in My Word, revelations embraced and held within your heart, line upon line, precept upon precept, all leading to the hidden riches of secret places, the sealed fountain of my End time wine vendors." And I understood that every stone was a small piece of understanding from the Word which touched other pieces of revelation, and when placed end on end, they paved the way to the place within where the end-time wine was waiting in the darkness. It was also clear that there are many such end-time scribes who have shared living water through their pens until now, but a fresh release of the wine of the Word was appointed them to steward. It would have dimension and structure and great substance and ignite change in all who drink of it. However, first they would need to spend time in the birthing room, being exposed to the contents of the wine and the ministrations of the zephyrs, until they understand and carry within them clear understanding of its structure and content, so that they can steward the wine well, bringing forth meat at the appointed time.

A zephyr is defined as 'a breeze that is westerly or gentle'. In Western tradition, the west wind is considered the gentlest or mildest of wind direction (blowing from the west in an eastward direction). When the warm west winds come, it indicates spring is near, so this wind brings a rain that awakens the plant life from its long winter sleep. The glass-smooth end-time wine in the large vat has been asleep, stored and waiting for its appointed time of awakening. The rainbow-colored zephyrs on its surface are warming and waking the wine. They are the gentle warm breezes of the seven spirits of God blowing deep within the wine cellar of the scribes.

According to the experts, brief exposure to air for a bottle of wine is beneficial, since it allows wine to breathe - similar to stretching its legs, or getting its circulation going, after being cooped up in the bottle for so many years. The breeze warming the surface of the wine assists in releasing aromas & opening the bouquet. As this end-time wine is dispensed through the pen of the ready writers, it forms part of the heavy latter rain, an eloquent impartation of God-breathed words, endued with the breezes of the seven spirits of God. Their words will awaken all that is sleeping within the hearts of the hearers and impart resurrection life. The wine scribes will release wine from Wisdom's table; it is the best wine reserved for the end-time army who ride behind their King.

Pro 9:5 Come, eat of my bread, and drink of the wine I have mixed.

In a recent article called 'Sought Out and Sent' (which can be found on my blog https://freshoilreleases.wordpress.com/), I spoke of the forging of a silver goblet belonging to the Bridegroom and shared how it contains the end-time wine. As I mentioned in the introduction, this silver vessel is used in the daily outpouring of wine during the Feast of Tabernacles and depicts the Bride of Christ, purified and forged in the refiner's fire and being displayed as His workmanship, created in Christ Jesus for the good works He has prepared for her to walk in.

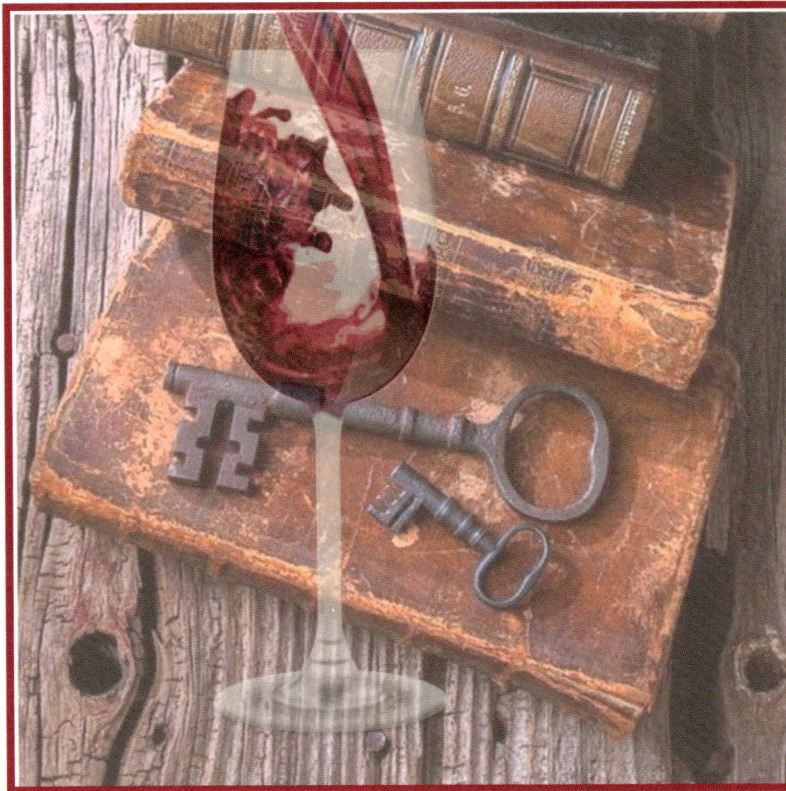

I see a multitude of wine-soaked books being released from the birthing room, containing words never heard until this time; revelations kept hidden until now and unveiled to impart light and truth to the end-time Bride. From the belly of the scribes, the best wine is about to flow. As the Bridegroom says about the Bride in Song of Songs:

Son 7:2 Your body is like a round goblet in which no mixed wine is wanting.

Chapter 2 ~ The Spring Wine is waiting

The day after the Lord showed me the end-time wine cellar, I was instructed to revisit it. When I stepped into the room, I could see there were dusty rows of wine bottles with corks lying on their sides. I wondered if they were empty, because I could not see the familiar dark red color of wine inside them. I went to have a closer look and to my surprise, I saw that each closed wine bottle contained a small rainbow-colored zephyr. Instantly I knew that these were applications of the seven spirits of God which had been held back and reserved for this time.

Then I saw a large sword come down, opening all the bottles in one swipe. The zephyrs in each one rushed out. They knew they had been released to dance in the wine vat, and I heard excited laughter which almost sounded like a group of schoolgirls, as they began dancing in the vat which contained the end-time wine. They looked as if they were trampling out grapes but actually, their movements were awakening and causing an undulation on the surface of the wine. It was strange as they should really have sunk into the wine but they were treading on the surface, so I assumed they were feather-light, yet somehow the 'weight' of their movement moved the wine considerably. I could see the wine was actually behaving like a solid. It had substance, could be measured and there were wave forms from the trampling, which were shaped like sound waves. I began to pray that I would be granted the right to hear what the zephyrs were releasing from The Lord's stored last day wine. Suddenly a phrase floated past my eyes. It was being spoken but I could also see the words. It said:

'FULL ROUNDED SOUND; SPRING WINE; LAST DAYS SIGNS AND SOUNDS'.

And I knew that those who drank of this wine would move in signs and wonders and be a part of releasing Heaven's sound in the earth, to bring the harvest to full ripeness so it could be brought in. To hear the wine called 'spring wine' was confirmation of what I had learned concerning zephyrs, as they are warm breezes from the West that herald the arrival of spring. So it made sense that the zephyrs would be warming the spring wine. What is important about the West wind is that it is mentioned once in the Word, in the context of being sent to deal with the devastating locusts in Egypt:

Exo 10:19 And the LORD turned a mighty strong west wind, which took away the locusts, and cast them into the Red sea; there remained not one locust in all the coasts of Egypt.

The zephyrs are feather-light but their impartation makes the wine mighty and strong like the wind that swept the locusts away. Joel 2 speaks of the Lord restoring the years which the locust has eaten. The end-time wine will carry a powerful anointing for restoration and realignment, for cleansing and reorientation, for recompense and release of inheritance. The Hebrew word translated 'West' is 'yam', also meaning 'to roar'. So this west wind contains the roar of the Lion of Judah. The treading of the zephyrs is imparting the roar into the wine, so that as it is poured out, great power is released. The zephyrs (which are applications of the seven spirits of God before the throne) are breathing into the wine, imparting life. The wine is becoming filled with the Spirit of Life; it is becoming packed with powerful, yoke-breaking anointing.

I began singing as I somehow knew that my new song in tongues would provide the music for the zephyrs to dance to. It is a wild tune that emerged; a 'shiggayon' is the word that floated past my sight (it is mentioned at the beginning of Habakkuk 3). I saw the zephyrs begin dancing steps like an Irish jig with high steps, treading powerfully on the surface of the wine and causing it to rise up in big waves and I briefly glimpsed again the shelves of books hidden within the end-time wine. So I knew that in this season we are entering, worship in the Spirit is key to revealing the contents of the end-time wine.

To those who are scribes, authors, songwriters or preachers, remember this as you visit the end-time wine cellar: You cannot share what you do not see. You cannot say what you do not hear. Our worship in unknown tongues causes the seven spirits of God to impart life and power to the contents of the wine vat and without their help; you cannot see and receive your instruction for the days ahead.

Shortly after the wild wine dancing began, I heard another string of words, which seemed like a set of steps that must be fulfilled:

'Unveil   Unseal   Reveal   Release   Resound'

When I asked the Lord what He meant by these words, He brought to my mind again the DNA spiral hidden in the wine and the shelves of books which had never yet been read. All these instructions concerned the opening and reading of these books. Then He said the words again one by one and as each one was sounded out, I saw and understood what was meant, and also knew that we need to pray and ask for each of these steps to be accomplished concerning the release of the details of our assignments for the year to come:

UNVEIL - take the covers off

Some shelves had dustcovers over them, so their existence was not known and I saw angels taking off these dustcovers and exposing the books underneath to the light. What was previously hidden, but present, began to come into plain sight. There were rows of books never seen or read by earthly eyes before.

UNSEAL – unlock

Some books had padlocks on them and needed keys to be inserted to open them. Others were in the form of scrolls which had wax seals which had to be broken so that the scroll could be unfurled, making it possible to open easily again and again. Until the key was given, the book's contents could not be read.

REVEAL – open

Once the unsealing had taken place, whoever was reading the book had to open the covers and then be shown what is contained within. I saw some of the books opened, but the pages seemed blank and then I knew that these portions of revelation were not mine to see or hear. Only the specific person to whom the revelation was appointed would be able to access the book's contents.

RELEASE - send forth the impartation contained within.

I saw that the revelation light contained in the book had to be imparted INTO the person for whom it was appointed; much like John was instructed to eat the scroll in the Book of Revelation. I saw the wine-colored words inscribed on the pages, plus the layout and dimensions of the book, flying off the pages and into the recipient. I also saw that sometimes the person would feel full and close the book and put it back on the shelf.

Then later, they would visit the wine cellar again and worship, before taking the book off the shelf that was revealed, find their place and continue where they left off. The time between visits was in order to fully digest and understand the contents which had been imparted. Finally the last page was read and received and the book was placed back in the DNA library on its appointed shelf.

It seemed the impartation had not caused the book to diminish in any way; almost as if this was an eternal library of books, which could be imbibed and yet remain intact. There remained a heavenly record even after the contents had been downloaded in the earthen vessel.

RESOUND -sound again

Once the words and sounds received in this birthing chamber have been digested, all that remains is to re-sound or repeat the sound you heard in the endtime wine cellar. As the words are repeated in the ears of those listening, the roar of the Lion of Judah is unleashed. Some books will be written down and published. Others will be preached.

Yet others will release powerfully anointed worship songs which usher in the glory realm of Heaven. Other books which are imparted will contain instruction for missions to other places and the words which must be spoken and the actions which must be fulfilled once there. All books in the end-time wine shelves will be for the last great harvest of souls. The Spring wind brings the Spring rain, which is the heavy latter rain that completes the harvest. The Hebrew word for 'latter rain' also means 'eloquence'. The books and writings of the end-time wine scribes will be eloquent, revelation-filled, wisdom-imparting, yoke-breaking powerhouses that cause seismic shift in those who read them or sing them.

Beloved, pray for last days wine to be warmed within, to be unveiled and awakened, unsealed, its contents revealed. Ask that the zephyrs would so move upon it that its DNA structure or hidden contents would be raised up to sight and light, so you can see and hear the sound of what is written in the volume of the Book of Last Days wine for you. As I have been doing this daily, there has been violent shaking and reverberation within, and a sound of roaring as the sound of the last days wine is warmed and released within my earthen vessel. Receive your end-time instructions, make time to sit and receive the sound of Heaven reserved for you for the time ahead. Then re-sound or sound again, say again what you hear said in the volume of the book. These are the wine fountains of the deep, and the fountain pens of the deep will release the wine-soaked words stored up and hidden for such a time as this. If you see it, you can say it. If your hear it, you can do it. Jesus told His disciples, "What I say to you in the dark, tell in the light; and what you hear whispered in the ear, proclaim upon the housetops" Mat 10:27. As the sound of the roar within the endtime wine is released; as you release the portion of the voice of the Son of God imparted to you, resurrection life and power will be the hearer's portion.

Joh 5:25 Truly, truly, I say to you that an hour is coming, and now is, when the dead will hear the voice of the Son of God, and the ones hearing will live.

The sound of the voice of the Son of God deep within the wine cellar carries within it the power of resurrection. Things long dead will awaken and rise up on their feet and begin to release the potential stored inside them. And once the sound of the end-time wine has done its work in you, you will be able to dispense it for others to be transformed.

Chapter 3 ~ In the Volume of the Book

When I first visited the end-time wine cellar, I was under the impression that the books I saw stocking the shelves of the DNA spiral within the wine vat referenced anointed authors being released on the scene. However, as the understanding I had began to fill out and gain more depth, I saw that those that had been referred to as 'wine scribes' were in fact, any bridal soul who was willing to surrender their tongues to become the pen of a ready writer. We all hold the power of life and death in our tongues and the Lion of Judah is looking for those who are willing to only say what they hear the Father saying. He needs trustworthy bondslaves in positions of governmental power, not self-opinionated renegades who use their tongues like the piercing of a sword. He wants bondslaves who don't lean on their own understanding but defer to Him in all things; first ascertaining the mind of Christ on a matter and then speaking forth into the atmosphere the words needed to change it. Only those who have been tried and tested and found trustworthy can be released to carry the end-time wine. Only silver vessels, fully surrendered vessels of honor, those who work as one with the Lamb, are used at the Tabernacles outpouring. They are those who have been found faithful with little in the past season, and are then released with authority over much.

When I saw the DNA spiral in the endtime wine displayed like a library with shelves of books, it seemed to be a revelation on its own, but then the Spirit connected it to another vision I was shown in November 2018, which was depicting a scene I didn't immediately understand. I was shown a library in Heaven and the shelves stretched

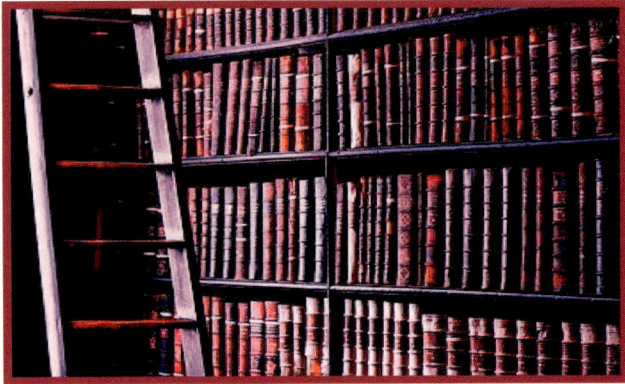

very high. I only saw one section in height but it seemed to stretch far up beyond my line of vision. There were angels on ladders, some changing and rearranging the places of books and others carrying scrolls, while still others sat writing in the books or scrolls.

Then my perspective of the scene changed and I saw that what I was viewing was a long length of DNA, and that it was actually the code sequences of the DNA that appeared as books on different shelves. These code sequence books were being taken out, opened, checked, bits added on blank pages, then closed, stamped and sealed with the Hebrew letter shin, before being replaced either where they came from or books were shifted along the shelves and the adjusted and sealed books were being put back in new places. The angels performing these tasks were messengers carrying out the instructions from the throne.

Some of the shelves were being dusted off and others had dustsheets pulled off them, and I was given the knowledge that these were very old books which had been silenced and hidden and their specific order represented muted codons (genetic sequences). I watched in fascination as windows were opened wide to let in more light on these books that had just been uncovered.

In the middle of the spiral library of shelves full of books, I could see a kneeling, praying figure. There was a cloud of fragrance rising off in coloured trails from this person and the angels would listen to the prayers and smell the fragrance rising and this seemed to tell them everything they needed to know about what to do next. The source of the prayers being uttered was the person's heart, where the Lord was enthroned. He or she was praying under the guidance of the Holy Spirit who had access to the deep things of God. Once the angels heard the instructions, they would move the ladders and access different books and go through the same process again. I understood that the shelves of books depicted the DNA of the person praying and that angelic messengers were doing genetic engineering, as the prayers ascended. All malfunction and broken places were being restored to order and correct sequence. I heard the word 'Restore' spoken as a command, but it was said like this: Re-Store, or store in different locations. The next word that was sounded out was 'Refurbish', then 'Re-open, Reveal, Reseal' and I knew that all these instructions concerned the angels working with the books on the shelves. I began to pray, "Lord let every codon in the library of my DNA receive Your mark. Let all the silenced books be uncovered and shine Your light on their contents. Let the sequence of the books in my DNA bring You glory."

The next scene I saw as I prayed were angels in a dormitory waking little children, who were sleeping in beds lined up like black and white piano notes. I knew somehow they were the sleeping DNA codons. "Why are they young?" I asked the Lord. "… Because they never had a chance to grow and mature. They were put to sleep at an early age," He explained. And I knew that these small children represented the books which had been asleep or hidden under dustsheets in the library. The arrangement of their beds like the keys of a piano indicated to me that each of these children had the ability to release a sound which was originally intended to be part of the music which came from the person whose DNA the library represented. "You have an orphanage inside of you," said the Lord, which startled me somewhat. "And all of them belong to you. Awaken them and embrace them as your own," He continued. David prayed for his inner self, his glory, to awaken, that this awakening of his whole being would in effect cause the dawn to come:

Psa 57:8 Awake, my glory (my inner self); awake, harp and lyre! I will awake right early [I will awaken the dawn]!

So I began to pray for the Lord to send angels to awaken every sleeping codon within my DNA and I declared that I embraced them as my own. I saw myself with my arms around the little group of children and asked God to complete the work He had begun in switching on the full complement of codons in the DNA sequence He had placed inside of me. Immediately I heard the words of a short poem that was announcing what effect the waking up of these codons would have in the spiritual realm:

'Sleeping beauty, waking queen, raised to power from your dreams, raised to glory, clothed with might, hidden weapon brought to light'

As I have pondered these words, I have come to realize that the work I saw going on in that giant library is not only being carried out in that one person praying, but in all appointed to be a part of the remnant Bridal Company. It is a foundational work done at cellular level, restoring the devastations of generations; bringing into alignment and full order in preparation for union with the Bridegroom. Transformation would precede elevation or ascension

Psalm 139 tells us that details about us are written in God's book before any of it manifested. I believe that what is being referred to as being written is the DNA sequence, which is carrying out the instructions within it and forming the embryo in the womb:

Psa 139:16KJV Thine eyes did see my substance, yet being imperfect; and in thy book all my members were written, which in continuance were fashioned, when as yet there was none of them. How precious also are thy thoughts unto me, O God! how great is the sum of them!

The words 'my members' does not actually appear in the Hebrew, so it actually says 'in Your book, all was written'. Now we know development does not stop once the baby exits the womb. Growth and change continue right through life and all of this is being done by the cells following the instructions written in the DNA. Having seen the angels working in the DNA library, it seems that some instructions are not heard because of the codons being muted or covered over. Therefore, some of God's thoughts toward us, or His plans and purposes for us, have yet to be heard or completed. The orphaned codons must be awakened and welcomed back into the fold so that the full rounded sound God intended our lives to make in the earth can be released. Once all our co-dons are firing and releasing their sound, the initial intended purposes of God which he encoded into our DNA can be carried out.

Ultimately, Jesus is the pattern Son, the DNA template from Heaven, which we need to fully align to, in order to be in full face to face union with Him. Only then can full fruitfulness come and God's spiritual blueprint for our lives be completely realized. Jesus is the Word made flesh; the spoken word from the mouth of God manifested in the earthly realm. He carried both the DNA of Mary, His mother, and the heavenly Y chromosome provided by the overshadowing of the Holy Spirit. I have no doubt that if the original Hebrew of the Old Testament was converted to a DNA sequence, one would have a representation of the Y chromosome Jesus carried.

When Jesus began His ministry, He stood up and read a portion of scripture and then declared that He was the manifestation of that Word. Psalm says this:

Psa 40:7 Then said I, Behold, I come; in the volume of the book it is written of me; Psa 40:8 I delight to do Your will, O my God; yes, Your law is within my heart.

This is then quoted in Hebrews 10, saying that Jesus spoke these words out:

Heb 10:7 Then I said, Behold, here I am, coming to do Your will, O God--[to fulfil] what is written of Me in the volume of the Book.

In the volume of God's book it is also written of us and the Pattern Son resides within us, so His codon sequence or RNA instruction is available to us (RNA is a single strand of nucleotide material). This is why Paul prayed for the Ephesians that the eyes of their understanding would be enlightened to know accurately the hope of their calling and THE GLORIOUS RICHES OF HIS INHERITANCE **IN** the saints.

That inheritance is what is written in God's book concerning His Son; the Pattern Son or the Template RNA strand. Perfect union and alignment means our own awakened DNA is joined as one to the Pattern Son. This awakening and reordering of the library of our DNA is the receiving of our end-time scrolls; the instructions written in the Book concerning Us. Once the codons are in divine order and healed and sealed with His Name, they begin to release the divine sound they hold within. We go from glory to glory by beholding Him; by beholding or gazing face to face; by our DNA scroll gazing as in a mirror toward the Pattern Son; a threefold cord that is not easily broken. No wonder Jesus said we would do even greater things. The rotating RNA rod of God, the Seed, the Son, is within us giving off light and sound from the volume of His Book and bringing forth the manifestation of Christ within us.

I had two other visions connected to the subject of DNA seven years ago and would like to share them here as they make more sense when placed against the background of the revelation recently received. On 1st July 2012, in worship, I saw two DNA strands fully winding round each other and it seemed as if it was a kind of intimate dance of sorts - I was given understanding that it depicted the conforming our wills fully to His spoken will written in the DNA of His express purposes for our lives, and that the Lord wanted us to lay aside every other plan and fully conform our wills to His will - even though we may not fully understand what exactly His unfolding will for us looks like. He wanted us to be like Mary, who really had little concept of the ramifications of what the angel told her was about to happen; yet she said, "Let it be unto me according to Your word."

The second vision I want to share happened a couple of months earlier, and because it also mentions a similar intimate dance, I sense it is connected to us fully aligning to what is written in the Book for us and in the process to the Pattern Son, our Bridegroom. It also explains the results of this union and perfect alignment in the earth and not coincidentally, makes mention of the zephyrs: During corporate worship on 20th May 2012, the day of a wedding ring solar eclipse (also called the ring of fire eclipse), we were singing a song with the words, 'where you go, I go, where you stay, I stay, God' and I realized that our wills were being conformed to the will of the Lord. I saw two fireflies but I could only see their red lights against a dark backdrop and they were following each other in a kind of dance.

Then I saw the Bridegroom and Bride on a rectangular dance-floor, similar to one found in dance competitions like 'So You Think You Can Dance'. At one end of the floor was a panel of sober looking judges and people were standing around the edge of the dance-floor in a large crowd and were watching them dance. One moment it seemed they were doing a waltz, next minute it was more like a tango and eventually it was hard to work out because it seemed to be no known dance and the judges were frowning but the Bride and Bridegroom were dancing flawlessly as one, the amateur with the expert, as she followed His confident lead. The people are watching in amazement and their faces become filled with wonder but, in absolute contrast, the judges' eyebrows were going up because they knew the laws about dancing and all the rules were being broken. They couldn't see the beauty of the dance because their vision was blurred by their knowledge of the written dance laws.

Then as the audience gazed enraptured, they began to fall on their faces round the dance floor and became sheaves of wheat that have been harvested. While this was happening, the judges were so busy deliberating and disqualifying the couple that they hardly noticed the sheaves, but then Jesus stooped down and wrote in the sand 'a perfect 10' and I knew He was the ultimate Judge whose opinion mattered. Then I looked up and saw sheaves falling out of heaven and these were the answers to prayers for unsaved loved ones who have been in the audience, watching the dance of the Bride with the Bridegroom, but who were not participating. They come forth as sheaves out of the tomb from the seed of the promises that have seemed to fall to ground and died.

Then we worshipped further and the music leader started singing about stepping out on the water of the Word and not being afraid and I looked again and saw the dance-floor was white and had writing on it and the bridal couple were dancing on the foundation of the written Word, but there was a gentle wind blowing around them, so the Bride was being led by the Spirit but supported by the Word. I heard the word 'zephyr' which I later found out means 'a gentle refreshing breeze'. As the Word says: '...*Not by might, nor by power but by my Spirit*'. Then our singing stopped and a man burst forth in prayer and praise and I heard the old song, ' a song shall be heard in the city of Judah and in the streets of Jerusalem, a song of joy, a song of gladness, a song of the Bridegroom, a song of the Bride'. I continued to see the dance-floor scene unfold.

The sheaves lying round the edges of the dance-floor got up and went onto the dance-floor. There seemed to have been an invitation issued for everyone willing to feel free to participate. Each one was dancing with their partner, yet somehow each one's partner was the Bridegroom - somehow they were all hearing their own song and doing different dances. It looked like a chaotic riot of color and movement from a horizontal level, but then I was elevated and given a view from above. From that vantage point, it was a glorious choreographed dance by the Lord of the Dance, almost like an orchestra playing with different instruments and parts and colors, like a giant kaleidoscope which the Lord was continuously turning with His hand and all the colored stones falling into different beautiful patterns, as they flowed without friction, suspended in clear oil. The point at which each person was hearing their own song speaks of the sound being released by their own DNA; fully restored and every codon functioning, and in perfect alignment with the Pattern Son. Let it be unto us according to Your Word! Some years ago, the Spirit gave me a song to release over myself. You may read the words opposite.

As our DNA, awakened and united with the Divine Seed, moves through the earth within our earthen vessel, the harvest will be brought in and the fullness of our God's eternal plan is carried out.

Sing Your song over me,
Creator of my soul.
Morning Star, sing for joy
As you come forth in me,
Let Your words of life caress
The heights and depths of all my soul,
'til every silent place awakes and sings.

And God said, "Let there be light",
And God said, "I will separate
The light from the darkness in you,
Live as a son of the Light."

And God said, "you are My seed,
Go forth and bear much fruit,
And as you abide in the Vine,
You'll bring forth fruit
After My kind."

And God said, "You are My bride,
Taken from under My side,
And the two shall be one,
Go forth and rule in the earth."

Honeyed oil
Does not spoil
Fresh oil from ages past
Is Mine
I come to give you
Honeyed wine
To permeate
And penetrate
Imbue
With dew
Anew
Hues of light
And fresh insight
Peals
Of ye old
Sound
Abound
And
Wrap around.
Ancient gates
Await.

Come penetrate
The portals
Of a bygone time
Inside My mind
It's here you'll find
The wisdom
For the darkest day
And light abounds
To show the way
To Wisdom's table
Freshly laid
For you
My dove
With all My love
A spread
Designed to activate
Your inner gates
And time won't wait
For you

So set aside,
Carve out the space
For you and I
To sit apace
And talk together
Face to face
Allow My breath
To stroke the face
Of all that lies
Asleep within
And dew will fall
On ancient ground
Whose ears
Have never heard
The sound
Of Life
Now let Me warm
The soil
That holds the seed
Of Greatness,

Veiled and still
Allow My will
To work the earth
Within your vessel
Turn the soil
And saturate
With oil
Fresh-pressed
And blessed
And stored within
The urns
Of clods unturned
My eye can see
Your destiny
Be still
And know that
I Am is here
I will be lifted up
And poured
From you
In days to come
Once all awakens...

Chapter 5 ~ Producing His Full Rounded Sound

Once again, I was praying about waking up the codons and the sleeping DNA strands and I saw a vision; angels again waking children sleeping in beds in a dormitory. These are the codon children I had seen before. This time, they stand in a row for roll-call to check that every one wakened is present. Then the angels press the feet of the children one by one and they release a musical note from rounded mouths, almost like a church organ pedal which causes the organ pipes to release their sound. The thought fills me that my earthen vessel is a cathedral and this huge choir of codons is supposed to be singing constantly, worshipping God by releasing the fullness of their individual sounds, but this whole dormitory I have just seen has been sleeping 'til now and so there has been a huge gap in the choir stalls. Consequently, I have not been able to release a full rounded sound into the spiritual atmosphere. I hear again the scripture about glorious riches of His inheritance from Ephesians 1. Paul says the eyes of my heart must be enlightened or opened and awakened to see and realize the hope of my calling.

The Hebrew word for 'eye' also means 'fountain', so the eyes of my heart are a fountain and these codon children that I now see for the first time are part of the glorious riches of His inheritance which has been put inside me. The sound they release is meant to complete the sound released from the fountain of my heart into the earth. His inheritance within me releasing its full sound is the co-heir part fully made known in the earthly realm. The glorious riches of His inheritance within is that 'everything we need for life and godliness' spoken of by Peter, but a spirit of slumber entered when Adam fell and left the garden and some of those codons were silenced.

2Pe 1:3 according as His divine power has given to us all things that pertain to life and godliness, through the knowledge of Him who has called us to glory and virtue

Did you see that? We have already been given it. The glorious riches of His inheritance spoken of in Ephesians 1 is already in the saints, but the eyes of our hearts have to be awakened to SEE it. And Peter gives us the key here – everything we have been given is accessed through knowing Him. The word in Greek for 'know' used here means 'full discernment, to become fully acquainted with'.

Face to face, as in a mirror...
Beholding Him, we are CHANGED from glory to glory.

Our DNA library is rearranged and restored and sealed with His Name. And we are transformed or 'clothed over' with our HEAVENLY DWELLING; our transfigured or changed tent or body; our inheritance, which has been stored up in Heaven for us – stored up UNTIL the appointed time of the scrolls being opened and read and manifested.

As the Spirit instructed me further on the sounding of the codons, I saw a strip of vertically positioned organ pedals of bright colors, blue, orange and red. When the organ pedal gets pressed, it releases its own bass sound that fills out the sound the upper keys release. The upper keys represent spiritual keys; things we have been taught by the Spirit along the way in our spiritual journey. I don't know if you have noticed, but the use of the spiritual keys we have exercised so far still has not brought forth complete manifestation of that which we are pressing toward. Just as in the functioning of an organ, the top keys and the pedals work together to produce the music written on the music sheet. Codons and spiritual keys work together to release the full rounded sound; the complete sound which God designed your life to release into the spiritual atmosphere. Once the codons have been woken up and lined up in the correct order with the help of the angels, the fullness of the intention of the Great Composer is heard in the earth. There is a symphony that has been written by Heaven that the earth has never heard, but now in this generation, it is going to sound forth. All the instruments in God's orchestra are taking their places and each is going to play skillfully at the appointed time in the musical score and heavenly music is going to wrap this old world around, releasing incredible power to transform and change those who hear it.

David wrote in the psalms, 'Let all that is within me praise His holy Name', that means every cell, every chromosome, every codon releasing the sound of the Word which came forth from God's mouth when He designed and framed you, before the foundation of the earth. You were destined to live for the praise of His glory and to do this with all that is within you, all that lies sleeping must be woken up and activated. The whole choir of codons must sing; the whole orchestra must play; every pedal on the organ of your heart must release its unique sound at the appointed moment. Then the glory of God will fill your temple and you will not be able to stand to minister, but will fall to your knees in adoration as you are filled with wave upon wave of the same power that raised Christ from the dead.

As I pondered this taking place, I could feel and hear singing deep within where my spirit is located. I saw an image of a small boy standing under the dome of a cathedral roof and it is him I hear singing with all his might and the waves of sound are rising like an ethereal mist and filling the space in the dome high overhead with layers of sparkling sound and after a while, the whole interior of the cathedral is filled with this mist or cloud of the manifest presence of God. The manchild within releases the full rounded sound which fills the whole temple with glory.

HEAVEN'S MAGNUM OPUS

During a prophetic gathering in 2018, in the open heaven atmosphere created by the worship, I began to see and hear what God was doing. Before me in the spirit, a woman in a white garment with her head covered was sitting and waiting on the Lord. She was facing to the left. Then a wind started blowing strongly round her and whipped her garment into a spiral, as if she was in the center of a tornado, moving anti-clockwise. Then the garment and head covering began to change color starting at the head, from white to indigo and violet and finally purple.

Then I saw the skirt of her garment being swirled round to the right and the woman's figure began to form a treble clef (hard to explain, but it looked like she was becoming the beginning of a sheet of music being written). Then I saw little black musical notes begin to flow out of her to the right. They were flowing around joyously all over the place, but not taking up any position on the lines of the music sheet. Then I was shown some type of hook with four points (in the shape of an X or cross), which I understood was for the purpose of fastening each note in its appointed place in the score, and I heard the following words:

Anchor me in Your melody
Let me be a part of Heaven's sound
Blow me into Your symphony
As it sounds and then resounds,
Blood-soaked chords of grace
Falling gently down
Chasing death
Where're it's found
Let Your roar reverberate
Through this temple that is Yours
Echoes of Your victory
It is done, battle won
I am free, Christ in me,
Saturate this earthly realm
With the sound of Heaven's rain
Pour it out and let it flow
Let us feel Your heart again...

Wrap this tired, old world around
With the strains of Yahweh sound,
Holy chords rise and fall
Heaven's wine poured out for all
Who thirst and bow before His feet
Throne-room plans are now complete,

Love's crescendo crashing down,
Wave on wave of power abounds.
Chains are broken, dead are raised
Lost ones found and God is praised.
Place me now and anchor me
In my place in Your symphony,
Cause my heart to know my place
In Your grand opera of Grace
As You breathe and send us forth
From this time before Your face.

What struck me in this image is that the woman who had made herself ready and been in a time of waiting, now had a mighty encounter with the wind or seven zephyrs of the Spirit and was not only turned to face forward, but her garment and mindset are changed to apostolic (purple) and she also became part of the new sound that God is releasing in this hour. This woman is the corporate Bride of Christ, whose transformation into the treble clef indicates a new piece of music is about to begin.

The musical notes which pour out from the belly of the treble clef represent the individuals who form part of the corporate Bride; previously hidden and in waiting, they now burst forth much like the disciples from the upper room, after a mighty encounter and infilling of the Spirit.

The prayer of the Bridal Company which I saw is to be anchored in each one's specific place upon the musical stave, in order for the full, clear sound of this piece of Heavenly music to be heard in the earth. Any confusion will result in a discordant sound being released, as notes are sounded out of time and place. This is Heaven's Magnum Opus; the grand finale sounded forth when the Father brings all things together in Christ:

That in the dispensation of the fullness of times he might gather together in one all things in Christ, both which are in heaven, and which are on earth; even in Him: In whom also we have obtained an inheritance, being predestined according to the purpose of him who works all things after the counsel of his own will: That we should be to the praise of His glory, who first trusted in Christ. Eph 1:10-12

The word 'stave' also means 'a strong stick, especially one that is used as a weapon' and comes from the word 'staff', which is a symbol of office or authority. This piece of music, when all notes are properly placed, becomes a weapon carrying authority in God's hand, as He uses Heaven's sound to create and manifest His will in the earth.

This is not so much about 'doing' as 'being'. We are moving from the Church age to the Kingdom age and we minister out of who He has made us to be; who we are in Christ, rather than what we do; it's about Christ in us being seen as opposed to us and our giftings being recognized. Giftings belong to the Church age; in the Kingdom Age, we release out of the manifestation of Christ within us; with all that is within us transformed and changed from glory to glory. It's not about ministry as much as Kingdom purposes being fulfilled.

When thinking of each musical note anchored in its appointed place on the stave, I am reminded of the stars accurately and precisely placed in the Heavens in their constellations.

Psa 19:1 To the chief musician. A Psalm of David. The heavens are recounting the glory of God, and the expanse proclaiming His handiwork. Psa 19:2 Day by day they pour forth speech, and night to night reveals knowledge. Psa 19:3 There is no speech, nor are there words where their voice is not heard.

The stars pour forth a form of speech or sound, but it is not heard by natural ears. As they remain anchored in their God-appointed positions, they recount the glory of God and reveal knowledge. In the same way, as you allow God to anchor you in His appointed position in the musical score, your surrendered, holy life releases a sound in the spiritual realm that contains great power – without one word coming out of your mouth. Each star on its own carries no message, but positioned within the constellations, a powerful message resounds and reveals the knowledge of God. One musical note on its own carries little meaning, but when placed in context with all the other notes exactly where God intends them to be, a glorious symphony of praise resounds throughout the earth.

One of the meanings of the word 'stave', when used as a verb is 'to release (wine, liquor, etc.) by breaking the cask or barrel'. This music that we are to become a vital part of is Heaven's best wine, formed from much crushing and maturing out of sight; the expression of the rich wine of His fierce love in a world where the wine has run out. Much like the woman who broke her alabaster box and the fragrance filled the whole house, this symphony poured forth from the Bride as the wind of the seven Spirits moves mightily within her, will fill the whole earth with the knowledge of the glory of the Lord and the fragrance of Christ.

The woman in my vision was turned or changed and transformed in such a way that the Spirit was able to release from within the sound appointed for a new era, transforming your focus to an apostolic mindset, and then carrying you to your appointed place on the stave. John the Baptist knew his position on the stave of his generation. When asked, he said he was 'the voice of one crying in the wilderness'; he was the sound preparing the way for the first coming of the Lord. He knew exactly where in the volume of the book it was written of him. He knew the hope of his calling. Nothing was asleep within him. He was fully activated and flowing in the destiny Heaven appointed him. In the same way, there is coming a release of a company who are the 'voice' or sound of a group of bondslave messengers, whose task is to prepare those who call themselves 'The Way' for the coming or manifestation of the Bridegroom within their midst.

The X shaped anchor I was shown in the vision of the musical notes coming forth from the woman in white is interesting. Tav, the last letter of the Hebrew alphabet was represented in ancient times by a pictograph shaped like an X. This final anchoring indicates the completion of the work of preparation in you. Jesus is the Alpha and the Omega; the Aleph and the Tav, and He who began a good work in you will bring it to completion in the Day of the Lord. This appointed place on the stave is what all your preparation and training has been about; what all the previous chapters have shaped and formed you for. You are His workmanship, created in Christ Jesus for good works which God has prepared beforehand for you to walk in.

Your position on the musical stave indicates exactly what God has made you to be. In Christ Jesus, your earthen vessel releases a beautiful, rich sound as you fulfill the call for which Christ took hold of you. This is what you have been pressing toward, to take hold of the fullness of your high calling. This is what all that refining has shaped you to be. This is your Tav, your swan song, your glorious part in the crescendo of Heaven's work in the earth; the part your instrument will sound forth in heaven's Magnum Opus.

Imagine my amazement when the speaker for the prophetic gathering stood up and announced the Lord had instructed her to call forth the women of the South to be part of Heaven's new sound! The south is also 'the right hand', so this is about coming forth to be a part of the sound of the sons of the right hand. What a powerful confirmation of all I had seen by the Spirit.

Chapter 4 ~ The Name of the Dead and their Inheritance

In the book of Ruth, there is the depiction of a profound spiritual truth concerning the Bride and the Bridegroom. Ruth finds herself gleaning in the fields of Boaz and when the barley harvest is taken to the threshing floor, she is given instruction by Naomi:

Rth 3:3 Wash and anoint yourself therefore, and put on your best clothes and go down to the threshing floor, but do not make yourself known to the man until he has finished eating and drinking.

The widowed Naomi tells Ruth to cleanse herself, perfume her body and dress in her best garments. Does that not sound to you like the Bride making herself ready?
She does this and then lies at the feet of Boaz and when He becomes aware of her, she basically asks him to marry her.

Rth 3:9 And he said, Who are you? And she answered, I am Ruth your maidservant. Spread your wing over your maidservant, for you are a next of kin.

The word for 'wing' means 'the edge of a garment' and refers to the ancient practice of a Bridegroom wrapping his Bride in his prayer shawl or talit once the vows have been spoken. The talit is a representation of his covering, protection and provision. Effectively, he is bringing her into his house. The reason she gave for making this bold request is that he was in a position to be her kinsman-redeemer. In ancient Israel, if a husband died, all his wealth and possessions were locked up in essence and his widow could not access them. The only way she could get them legally released was to marry her husband's brother or failing that, another close relative. Then the child born of their union would be known as the 'firstborn from among the dead' and would re-ceive an inheritance both from his biological father and his mother's dead husband. In other words the double portion is the right of the firstborn from among the dead. Ruth would be provided for and protected by her husband Boaz, having released the locked up inheritance to her firstborn.

The whole process was to be initiated by a secret betrothal in the darkness of the night. Boaz knows Ruth's reputation and character and promises to do for her all she asks but he knows another closer relative who has a superior claim. So he has to go to the city gates to deal with the matter. as this is where all legal issues are dealt with. However before he does this, in the darkness of the early morning watch, he asks Ruth to hold up her mantle and he pours 6 measures of barley into it. That is a heavy download! He then instructs her to take it home to her mother-in-law.

What is depicted here is a secret tryst in the night of a new day in the Bride's life. Je-sus is our Kinsman-Redeemer Bridegroom. Her mantle, which depicts her calling and anointing, is imbued or filled with 6 more measures of barley to add to the one meas-ure she gleaned by herself. Bar is the Aramaic word for son, in the sense of an heir, as opposed to the Hebrew 'ben', which is a son in the sense of building a family. So the bar-ley download here depicts the receiving of a stored up inheritance. Now we know that Ephesians 1:18 says the glorious riches of our Kinsman-Redeemer's inheritance is found IN the saints. Ruth had seen and experienced one measure of inheritance, but stored up in Heaven's accounting books is a vast outpouring of 6 measures which can only be released to her once she is face to face and alone with her Bridegroom-to-be, and has forged the beginning of the Bridal covenant.

In a flash, she receives a download into her mantle of what is written in the volume of the Book or the storehouse of the Kinsman-Redeemer. Now she possesses 7 measures of inheritance, the fullness of inheritance; measured portions of the seven spirits of God imparted into her mantle. Veiled and sleeping codons are awakened and the Bride is changed. From this time on, she will not be known by her own name but as the wife of the Kinsman-Redeemer. This is why Naomi asks her a strange question when she arrives home, laden with barley.

Rth 3:16 And she came in to her mother-in-law. And she said, Who are you, my daughter? And she told her all that the man had done to her.

"Who are you?" The face to face encounter in the early morning watch has transformed Ruth from glory to glory. She does not look like the same person. She has left the house of her dead husband and joined the house of the Kinsman-Redeemer, but still the legal marriage has to take place in the gates. The action of marrying a widow was known as 'restoring the name of the dead to their inheritance'. The nearer relative declares that he isn't prepared to marry Ruth because she was of Moab, which means 'of my father', a tribe begun by a daughter's incestuous union with her father Lot. But Boaz knows that Ruth was a woman of valor and does not display the characteristics of the genetic strain from which she came forth. So he makes a decree in the gates of the House of Bread, Bethlehem:

Rth 4:9 And Boaz said to the elders and all the people, You are witnesses this day that I have bought all that was Elimelech's and all that was Chilion's and Mahlon's, from the hand of Naomi. Rth 4:10 And also Ruth of Moab, the wife of Mahlon, I have purchased to be my wife, to raise up the name of the dead on his inheritance, so that the name of the dead may not be cut off from among his brothers and from the gate of his place. You are witnesses this day.

There are a number of important truths to glean out of his words. The inheritance of the dead fathers and sons is purchased or redeemed by the Kinsman-Redeemer. That land can now be sown with seed, watered and a crop harvested. The gleaner Ruth is now his wife and resurrection power is at work to 'raise up the <u>name</u> of the dead on his inheritance'.

The Hebrew word for 'name' also means 'character, authority'. In your DNA are covered places, sleeping codon sequences; dead places where no sound is heard. The decree released in the gates resurrects what is silent and beyond access. The character and authority inscribed in your muted codons will again begin to sound forth. The fullness of godly inheritance which has been locked up in your earthly line will now be restored to full function. The places where death has been at work in your genetic makeup are now flooded with resurrection life and light. This is what the angels were doing in my vision when they took dustsheets off bookshelves and opened windows to let the light flood in.

The other thing the kinsman-Redeemer decrees that he prevents is that *'the name of the dead may not be cut off from among his brothers'.* In other words, that which is endued with God-given authority and character shall be manifested in the midst of the brethren, or the Body of Christ. For a long season, those particular codons and parts of the DNA structure containing inheritance have been muted and chained up because of legal issues in the spiritual realm. But now, full union and marriage to the Kinsman-Redeemer results in liberation and complete expression and manifestation as the Father originally intended. The locust has eaten too many years and now the Kinsman-Redeemer decrees recompense and restoration of full inheritance and capacity to bless the Body of Christ though your unique abilities and design.

No-one else has the DNA you contain. You are a one of a kind vessel, intended to live for the praise of His glory and the early morning watch download of barley seed will be digested and unpacked and begin to fill your whole body with light as it releases its nutritious content into the depths of your being. Every joint will supply as God intended in His end-time army of bondslave lovers, because they are fully joined to the Head, the Bridegroom, their Kinsman-Redeemer.

The third result of the marriage to the Kinsman-Redeemer is that the name or authority of that which is dead will not be cut off 'from *the gate of his place'*. What does this mean in plain English? Well, in God's kingdom plans and distribution of inheritance and individual portions, it is intended that at the age of adoption (or the setting in place of a son which was at age 30 in the natural), you should be granted the right to enter through certain gates or portals in the spiritual realm, in order to be able to stand in your appointed place for end-time ministry to carry out your Father's business.

We see this whole principle of the Kinsman-Redeemer operating being enacted in the Book of Zechariah. Joshua the high priest has been plucked as a brand from the fire and in spite of the accusations of satan before the throne, God declares that He chooses Jerusalem, in spite of Joshua's filthy garments (just as Boaz chose Ruth from her unclean background). Then new rich garments are brought and a clean turban is wrapped around his head. In other words, Joshua is clothed over or transformed; the clean turban representing the total renewal of his mind with heavenly thoughts and instructions. Then the Lord declares:

Zec 3:7 Thus says the Lord of hosts: If you will walk in My ways and keep My charge, then also you shall rule My house and have charge of My courts, and I will give you access [to My presence] and places to walk among these who stand here.

Joshua is given access to the place of His presence; to the place before the throne. IN other words, God has planned for Joseph to be able to enter the gate or spiritual portal that brings him right before the throne. He is also granted 'places to walk', spiritual territory to traverse amongst those who are granted to stand before the throne and see Him face to face. Joshua's name is not removed from the gate of his place in spite of satan's accusations. The thief's words of death and faultfinding have been effectively silenced or muted and Joshua is moved to a different spiritual portion; no longer is he in the refiner's fire but granted places of spiritual authority to stand in.

Every one of his codons is releasing its sound and he will be operating in fullness of power, that incomparably great power available to us as believers once we have accessed the fullness of our inheritance. Joshua has also been granted the ministrations of the seven spirits of God – one stone with seven eyes. All that remains is the crowning ceremony and then there is full release to rule as a co-heir.

So to bring it back to a more personal level, the glorious riches of His inheritance in me is released progressively by accepting the Bridal price paid for me with His broken body and Blood. Every time I partake in communion, I am declaring over myself that the Kinsman-Redeemer has spread His wing over me and that within the fullness of His inheritance which will be downloaded to me is those 6 measures of barley, the 6 measures of the remaining 6 spirits of God that accompanies my full redemption.

I break bread every morning and thank the Lord for spreading His wing over me, for sharing His inheritance with me. I hold out my hands and in faith declare that I am holding out my widow's mantle to receive the downloading of those 6 measures of the Spirit. This is my portion of allotted inheritance and I thank Him that the RNA strand of the Pattern Son is releasing all within me that has been locked up or muted, that every sleeping codon is awakened to sound forth the fullness of my destiny. I embrace all that the Living Word is within me and decree that in every place in my body, soul and spirit that is without form and void, light is entering and resurrection power is working.

And I thank my Kinsman-Redeemer for speaking in my gates. I thank Him for releasing His sound and breath into the eyes and ears of my heart. It is the release of the breath of the Bridegroom carrying His sound in the gates that completes the full redemption transaction. Each time I break bread, there is an awakening of the inheritance in me; switching on and activating more of my inheritance which has been sleeping inside me all along!! I pray intentionally for God to show me great and mighty things that I know not; for the eyes of my heart to be enlightened to know in detail what the glorious riches of His inheritance are for me; that I may see and hear what is written in the volume of the book (in the divine DNA code) for me to fulfil and accomplish. That 6 measures of barley seed is not eaten all in one day; there is a progressive unfolding and revealing of the parameters of our downloaded inheritance. We are His workmanship, created in Christ Jesus for good works, which God has prepared and encoded and written for us to walk in! We just need the blueprints to be opened for us to read in full.

After the fullness of redemption is resounded in the gates and the transaction legally recorded, then comes the blessing by the guests standing round, followed by consummation (full union) and fruitfulness.

And Obed, the manchild brought forth from union with the Kinsman-Redeemer walks in a double portion of inheritance as part of the company of the Firstborn from among the dead. This includes resurrection power and authority and the ability to impart release and recompense to others as they go about their Father's business. Obed means 'bondslave'. Those who are the bondslaves of the Lamb; who follow Him wherever He goes are that firstfruits company seen on Mount Zion. They are the ones who sing a new song, the song of the end-time wine.

Chapter 5 ~ The SoundTrack of the Birthing Room

I am back in the endtime wine-cellar and it is not quiet like last time I was here. There seem to be words floating round in the air and I realize that they must have been released by the zephyr's trampling of the wine. I hear them as they zip past me; they all seem unconnected and yet they contain profound meaning concerning God's last days intention through this wine release. In fact, they don't seem to have the usual English dictionary meanings at all, but I am hearing the explanation of the meaning of these words as they float past me making their sound, and some of them, I have never heard before. I will list them as I heard them and then expand on the understanding I was given concerning each strange phrase:

'Waken' but it has a hyphen: Way-ken
- I know your ways, I have seen where you have walked and I will heal you.
The sound released through the end-time wine will bring realignment and healing for every crooked path and misunderstanding. Truth will be the plumbline used as a standard.

'Breakin' Records'
– there will be a breaking of DNA records of Dionysus and Dagon. Dagon be gone!
In sections of our DNA code, there is interference and false records which have been inserted, so that when the sound is released from that section of codons, there is a misrepresentation and therefore wrong manifestation or sound waves which come forth.

The enemy loves to muddy the waters flowing from our vessels and the end-time wine will remove and delete all records which shouldn't be in the bookshelf of your DNA. This phrase that I heard really struck me: 'Dionysus debarred, Dagon demoted'. So without really understanding all the implications, by faith I began to decree these two statements or judgments over myself. A strong anointing hit me and I began to tremble deep within. I knew something was being broken which had resisted the fullness of God's intention coming forth. Later I did some research and what I discovered was astoundingly relevant to the topic of the endtime wine.

Dionysus is the god of the grape-harvest, winemaking and wine, of fertility, ritual madness, religious ecstasy, and theatre in ancient Greek religion and myth. Originally a god of the fertility of nature, associated with wild and ecstatic religious rites, in later traditions he is a god of wine who loosens inhibitions and inspires creativity in music and poetry. He is also called Bacchus. This demonic prince is the maker of the counterfeit wine of the Babylonian system that brings forth all that is soulish and fleshly in the Church. He will resist and try to quench any flow of Divine creativity that is intended to have a powerful impact for the Kingdom. He resists the downloading of divine inspiration, inhibits and interferes with creative flow and the completion of a God-given vision for a creative project.

Dagon was an ancient northwest Semitic god worshiped by the early Amorites and by the people of Ebla and Ugarit. He was also a major god, perhaps the chief god, of the biblical Philistines. King Saul's head was displayed in a temple of Dagon. The attack by this evil spirit will try to muddy your prophetic creative flow with fleshly interpretation and religious restraint. It is the ark of God positioned in the temple of Dagon that causes that principality to lose its head or influence upon your mind.

As I am writing this passage, I am reminded of one day during the preparation for the downloading of the revelation of the endtime wine cellar. I was in prayer and asked the Father that any interference or resistance to the downloading of revelation He had for me be removed. Instantly I saw an obstruction in the second heaven between me and the Throneroom. It looked like a metal grating and as there was an outpouring of a liquid containing various jewels above my head, the metal grate caught the jewels and all I received was the diminished liquid. I got so angry that I began to pray in tongues like a wild woman. I decreed that every obstruction to me receiving the fullness of my portion was to be torn apart and removed and I served notice on every demonic entity tasked with keeping that grating in place. I resisted the thief who came to steal, kill and destroy my creativity and weaken the force of my contribution to the Kingdom of God.

As I prayed in this manner with a mighty zeal imparted by the Holy Spirit, I saw the grating tear in two, much like the temple curtain, and the demons that were holding the edges of the grating in place fled at top speed. Then I prayed the covering of the Blood upon my meeting with the Lord and asked for the fullness of the gems of revelation intended for my portion to be restored to me. This book is part of the answer to that day of fierce warring in the Spirit. Dionysus and Dagon will not touch or contaminate in any way the endtime wine which the silver vessel pours out!

'Bearing Fruit'

- of Heaven's sound, not earths re-bound sound.

For too long, the messages that have been passed around in church circles have just been echoes bouncing from earthen vessel to earthen vessel. Very little original release of the words from God's mouth has been heard. Now, through the end-time wine, fresh manna from the lips of the Lord will be released in the earth. And because it is endued with the zoe breath of God, great fruitfulness will come forth from vessels who embrace and hold fast this fresh bread from heaven's bakery.

'Finite In-finite'

– there will be a framing of infinite sound into finite bytes for earthly release.

Concepts and revelation which exist in the realm of eternity will be packaged in small pieces so that it can be heard and absorbed in the realm of time. Small sips of the end-time wine will provide line upon line, precept upon precept until the whole eternal, infinite truth being revealed is absorbed and understood.

'In – turnal E-turnal'

- Eternity is turning and changing you internally.

Eternity is in our hearts and as heavenly revelation is released within, it triggers transformation and transfiguration. We become less and less earthly and more and more heavenly.

'In-fernal'

- this new sound is from the wine cellar inside us, down below, the fountains of the deep within (from Latin *infernus* meaning 'below, underground').

This flowing revelation carries a sound not heard in the earth before. It is the best wine held back for the end time. It will be poured forth from living stones that have long held the waters of purification within, walking in the fear of the Lord.

'Phonetic Not-yet-ic'

– the release of sound which has never been heard or written about before, from eternal places in the Spirit that have never been seen before.

It is revelation sealed and stored up for this time and its effect upon the ears of man will be profound.

Joh 5:25 Truly, truly, I say to you that an hour is coming, and now is, when the dead will hear the voice of the Son of God, and the ones hearing will live.

'Re-urn-al'

– I saw a vessel being reformed and redecorated internally.
Some vessels have been marred in the making and at this time, the seven Spirits of God will employ the sound waves in the end-time wine released to forge and frame a new vessel or urn from the same building blocks of DNA. There will also be a furnishing with all weapons and equipment necessary to fulfill the purpose the new vessel has been fashioned for.

'Creative Ex-press-ion'

- a forming and pressing from without by the sound waves are shaping the vessel, like God formed Adam from the mud.

We have borne the image of the earthly and now the image of the heavenly will be impressed upon the face of our hearts

'Minting Coinage'

- these are those who have been framed or pressed into Heaven's desired shape by the sound waves of the atmosphere of Heaven released from the endtime wine; they are imbued with authority as heavenly coins, carrying a weight of glory and are the hidden riches of the secret places!!

'Heaven's Current-see'

- these have seen and heard what Heaven is currently saying and doing and so can be released to transact as heavenly currency in the earth. They say or re-release the sound they have heard from the Father's mouth and only engage in transactions they know Heaven is invested in. The time of dead works is over.

'7- single sound'

- the new sounds released from the vessels contain the impartation of the seven Spirits of God; individual rounded soundings.

A fresh new sound from the vessel is poured out for a new season; each release is unique, according to what is written in the volume of the Book for each one. In God's end-time army, no-one will be doing covers of someone else's sound.

All these unusual words quantify the effect of the sound waves of this wine that has been held back and reserved until the last time. Did you know that sound profoundly affects the surface it falls on. Sound is wave energy moving thru a medium. In contrast, light is electromagnetic energy which needs no medium, it can travel through the vacuum of space, and it behaves like discrete packets (quanta) of energy, as well as behaving like a wave. Sound doesn't come in packets and it has no existence apart from the medium it's moving through. This is why our vessels are needed – to hold and release the roar of the end-time wine!

I used to think God made Adam with His hands like a potter makes a vessel on the wheel. However, I am now considering the distinct possibility that Adam was formed from the action of the sound waves emerging from God's mouth on the mist-soaked earth. Sound has creative ability. So, in the endtime wine cellar within, the sound is released as the zephyrs move through the medium of the wine. Without the medium of the end-time wine, you would not be able to hear what God is saying to you. Heaven's sound brings heaven's light and fresh sight and understanding.

When we speak, our breath propels or pushes the sound waves carrying our words out of our mouths and through the medium of the air into the ears of our hearers. I had the privilege the other day of being shown the breath of the Lion of Judah in minute detail. It was composed of vibrating golden particles of dew full of resurrection power and molecules of living water; the wind of the Spirit imbued with them is a vehicle to carry His words of power to our hearts.

Remember when God formed Adam, he was a lifeless clay sculpture on the ground until the breath of God entered him. That Divine breath has the power to raise up all that is lifeless; all that has fallen to the ground within you.

Isa 26:19 Your dead shall live; the bodies of our dead shall rise. You who dwell in the dust, awake and sing for joy! For Your dew [O Lord] is a dew of [sparkling] light [heavenly, supernatural dew]; and the earth shall cast forth the dead [to life again; for on the land of the shades of the dead You will let Your dew fall].

These ones who offer themselves willingly are flowing forth as holy musical notes out of the womb of the dawn. Psalm 110 AMP calls them the young men who are as the dew! Each one embodies a heavenly sound; carries a message and resurrection power within their mouths. On the land of the shades of the dead, Your dew will fall. Your dew is the dew of sparkling light. The light-bringers are being released from the womb of the morning, bearing light because they have been filled with light; able to pour it forth because fullness of light has been poured into them. Remember you have to drink in His words before you can speak out His words.

Feather-light,
zephyr-bright,
still small Voice,
your choice
to stay and see,
to change and be
glorified,
all light inside,
city set,
upon a hill,
a place to which
others will
come and drink,
bathe and think,
and twinkling change,
and rearrange
will be the order,
of the day...

Your words
hold sway,
amidst the palsied
prophets
of the fading day,
Dionysus' demented
servant seed,
satan's breed,
soon 2B silenced
so I Am can speak
unhindered;
his license
rescinded,
operations cease.
My sounds
Increase
In volume
And measure...

My treasures
Released
To be
Sound doctrine
Sure light
And insight,
My might.
Bright warriors
Emerging
From the night
Of trial,
Tested vessels
Sealed and sent
Softly.
Dawn dew
Alighting
worldwide
With weighty words
Of light

Mount Zion's
Messengers
Sons of the morning
Melchizedek's seed
Ruling rod
They are
My scepter
Extended
In the midst
Of My foes

Chapter 6 ~ Wine-Pierced Bondslave Priests

The members of the barley firstfruits company are bondslaves to the Lamb. It is the ear that is pierced in the making of a bond slave. The instrument used for this ancient practice was an awl, as the ear lobe was held against the door frame.

Exo 21:6 his master shall bring him to God, and one shall bring him to the door, or to the doorpost; and his master shall pierce his ear with an awl, and he shall serve him forever.

The Hebrew word for awl is 'martsea', spelled mem, resh, tsadi, ayin.

Mem depicts the revealed truth of God.
Resh depicts the head, or ruler or the mind of Christ.
Tsadi depicts righteousness and is connected to the Melchizedek order.
Ayin depicts the eye or a fountain.

So the action of the awl is opening the ear and awakening it; opening the way for the revealed secrets and truth of the mind of Christ to be imparted to the righteous, The awl is a tool in the hand of the Master of the House, depicting a company of those who possess within them the revealed truth of God and the mind of Christ. This is the Melchizedek priesthood, who open the ear of those offering themselves willingly in the Day of His Power (psalm 110), thereby causing them to see or understand, because those who make up the tool of the awl are a fountain of wisdom and truth.

Notice also that the one being inducted as a bondslave is brought to *'the door, or to the doorpost'*. Obviously they are in the same place, but it is significant that both are mentioned. The one is part of the other. Let us deal first with 'the door', in other words, the servant who wants to become a bondslave is brought to Jesus, Who is the Door. It is He Who is made unto us wisdom of God. We must open our ear to His words and drink in the wisdom He shares with us. This will equip us to go forth as bondslave harvesters, governing and ruling in wisdom as we bring in the harvest for the Kingdom.

Isa 50:4 [The Servant of God says] The Lord God has given Me the tongue of a disciple and of one who is taught, that I should know how to speak a word in season to him who is weary. He wakens Me morning by morning, <u>He wakens My ear</u> to hear as a disciple [as one who is taught].

The word translated 'God' in Exodus 21:6 is actually 'Elohiym', a plural word which not only means the 3-in-1 God but also 'judges, angels or rulers'. So those who offer themselves willingly are also brought to those who have been counted trustworthy to rule and judge righteously; the overcomers which the Book of Revelation speaks of in the letters to the seven churches.

They are also depicted by the TWO doorposts, who are part of the Door-WAY, in which the DOOR is housed. The unyielding support and stability of the doorpost makes the action of the awl possible. The earlobe is actually positioned between the doorpost and the awl in order to bring forth a bondslave; once again TWO companies who carry within them the mind of Christ and the wisdom of Elohiym. There is another word which can be translated 'doorpost' and it appears in Isaiah 61:3. It is the word 'ayil', which appears as 'terebinths' (or 'oaks' in some translations). It can also be translated 'rams or chiefs':

Isa 61:3 To appoint unto them that mourn in Zion, to give unto them a garland for ashes, the oil of joy for mourning, the mantle of praise for the spirit of heaviness; that they might be called terebinths of righteousness, the planting of the LORD, wherein He might glory.

The terebinth tree grows to 40 meters and is found mainly in Jordan. In Jewish thought, when a man reaches 40, he is considered wise enough to judge righteously. The 'ayil' of righteousness are also the 'rams' of righteousness or the 'door posts' of righteousness or the 'leaders' who are righteous ie. The Melchizedek priesthood, kings or leaders of righteousness. Ayil is written aleph, vav, lamed.

Aleph- leader, chief

Vav – the connecting of heaven to earth, a nail

Lamed – the staff (of the bread of the Word

So ayil embodies the idea of the chief or leader who connects heaven to earth with his bread; in other words, it is a picture of Melchizedek who brings forth the bread and wine of heavenly revelation to nourish the seed of Abraham.

Joh 1:51 And He says to him, Truly, truly, I say to you, From now on you will see Heaven opened, and "the angels of God ascending and descending" on the Son of Man.

Jesus was the Heavenly Bread, the terebinth, leader, ram or chief, that came from Heaven to earth in order to connect them, and now we are entering the season when we will see 'angels' or messengers ascending and descending on the DNA pattern son, bringing portions of bread and wine from within library of the heavenly Pattern Son (which contains all that is written in the volume of the Book).

The ayil of righteousness in Isaiah 61:3, those who are 'planted' (which comes from a Hebrew root meaning 'to strike in, to fix, fasten'), are fixed (or anchored) by Yahweh in the musical score. They are the 'angels' or messengers who bring impartation of heavenly things because they are fixed or planted in heavenly places in the Spirit, even as they walk the earth.

Let's return to the picture of the willing one being brought to the door or the doorpost. A Door is found within the boundaries of the doorposts. In other words, the revelation of the Door, Christ, is found within or 'inside' –or amongst - the doorposts. This is why the company being marked as bondslaves must have their ear opened by the sound released from the doorpost. The doorposts carry within them the measure of the stature of the fullness of Christ.

THE REVEALING OF HIS JEWELS

Mal_3:17 And they shall be Mine, says the Lord of hosts, in that day when I publicly recognize and openly declare them to be My jewels (My special possession, My peculiar treasure). And I will spare them, as a man spares his own son who serves him.

The word 'serves' in the above verse refers to the ministrations of a bondslave. Remember in psalm 110 that it speaks of those who offer themselves willingly in the day of Your power? A bondslave is a slave who has been set free in the seventh year after being purchased by his master. He willingly submits himself to be pierced and serve His master for the rest of his earthly days. The Bride is a priestly company of bond-slave lovers of the Bridegroom.

At ordination, the priests had the blood of the lamb put on the lobe of their right ear in the same place as a bondslave was pierced with the awl. So it is the sound of the Blood that pierces through the bondslave's ear.

Lev 8:22 And he brought the other ram, the ram of consecration, and Aaron and his sons laid their hands upon the head of the ram. Lev 8:23 And Moses killed it and took some of its blood and put it on the tip of Aaron's right ear, and on the thumb of his right hand, and on the great toe of his right foot.

The Hebrew word translated 'consecration' means 'a fulfilling, (literally) a setting (of gems)'. The applying of the Blood on the right ear, right thumb and right toe depicts the hearing of the sound released by the DNA of God within the Blood of the Ram of Consecration, and the subsequent setting apart as a son of the right hand, walking only wherever the Lamb goes. This application of the Blood(and the sound it re-leases) completes the setting in place of the priesthood. This is the adoption as sons; the release of authority to function in our Father's business. The Blood of our Ram carries and imparts the authority we will be carrying.

The word for 'ram' used here in Leviticus 8 also means 'terebinth, oak, mighty man'. The Ram Jesus is also the Lamb, because He is fully surrendered to His Father's will and those 144000 who follow the Lamb wherever He goes also have the Lamb nature. They are bondslaves, fully yielded forever.

The oak (or 'ayil') wine barrel in the endtime wine cellar is also made up of oak planks, oaks of righteousness, terebinths of righteousness, the planting of the Lord. So the oak wine vat symbolizes the equipping of mighty men ministries to walk the earth in the time of the last great harvest. Hearing the sound of the DNA of God in the endtime wine is the same as reading in the volume of the Book the blueprint for you to carry out. Both John the Baptist and Jesus knew what was written in the volume of the Book for them to complete.

DEW OF HEAVEN

During the days of receiving the download for this book, I was praying for the dew to fall on the land of the shades of the dead one morning. I was shown a sleeping child lying on its back in a bed with neatly folded sheets, and dew is falling on the face of this child. It is sparkling, filled with light. I see it sink in to the child's face and there is an angel bending over the child, watching the progress. Each day, more dew falls and sinks in and then suddenly the child opens its eyes and sits up. I am reminded of the almond tree which is the first to awake after the winter. While all the other trees are still asleep it suddenly buds and blossoms overnight. Then the Spirit spoke, "It takes seven days of dew for awakening. On the seventh day, full healing and rising comes." Immediately a scripture came to mind:

Isa 30:26 Moreover the light of the moon shall be as the light of the sun, and the light of the sun shall be sevenfold, as the light of seven days, in the day that the LORD binds up the breach of his people, and heals the stroke of their wound.

The light of one day is as the light of seven days in the day that the Lord binds up your wounds. In this day, He is releasing the light and revelation of seven days (a complete season of preparation or consecration) to make us whole and heal the breach. What is the breach? It is the distance brought about between you and God by sin; both that of Adam and your own. When the breach is healed by this sevenfold light (the light released by the seven Spirits of God), all the codons wake up and rise up to release the sound God programmed into them when He designed you.

As I continued praying in tongues, the word, 'shakar' kept being repeated and I would see the almond tree as this word flew out of my mouth. The word 'shakar' means 'dawn, dayspring, early, morning, to rise up'. I was praying in tongues for my codons to wake up and rise up! David prayed similarly:

Psa 57:8 Awake, my glory (my inner self); awake, harp and lyre! I will awake right early [I will awaken the dawn]!

David speaks of his glory awakening before the dawn and influencing the coming of the dawn!! Aaron's rod lay before the presence of the Lord all night (like Ruth laying before Boaz) and in the morning it had been imbued with resurrection life, budded, blossomed and borne fruit, even though it was completely disconnected from the root which originally brought it forth. What caused this amazing phenomenon? The She-kinah presence of God woke up all the codons lying sleeping in the DNA of the cells in that almond rod and they began working and manifesting what they were divinely designed to bring forth. They were connected to the heavenly rather than their original earthly root. Before this unveiling in the light of morning, God had made a decree:

Num_17:5 And the rod of the man whom I choose shall bud, and I will make to cease from Me the murmurings of the Israelites, which they murmur against you.

Many are called but few are chosen after the examination of their hearts. Aaron had the blood of the ram on his ear lobe, right thumb and toe. The sound that released never fell to the ground even though the blood eventually wore off that consecrated ear. The sound penetrated the layers of Aaron's body and was stored in the cell memories, which are like detailed archive records. God chose Aaron because the sound of the blood could still be heard within his consecrated body.

Num 17:8 And the next day Moses went into the Tent of the Testimony, and behold, the rod of Aharon for the house of Levi had sprouted and brought forth buds and produced blossoms and yielded [ripe] almonds.

The word translated 'bud' also means 'to break forth, to fly' and the word 'blossom' can also be translated 'a wing'. It sounds like wings are growing in preparation for taking flight. The root of the name 'Levi' means 'to cleave, to unite, to remain'. The rod of those who have cleaved to Him; who remain in His presence and become filled with His resurrection breath will bud, blossom and bring forth fruit overnight. It is the manifest presence of God and the atmosphere contained therein that brings awakening and change.

Just like Aaron's rod, the menorah also has knops/buds, blossoms and the lit flame displayed as the ripe fruit (Exodus 25). However, until the oil is lit, no fruit is visible. The baptism of fire is essential.

Jer 1:11 Moreover, the word of the Lord came to me, saying, Jeremiah, what do you see? And I said, I see a branch or shoot of an almond tree Jer 1:12 Then said the Lord to me, You have seen well, for I am alert and active, watching over My word to perform it.

God was making a play on words when He spoke this as the root of the word for 'almond', 'shaqad', means to be alert, to be on the lookout'. The budding and blossoming of the almond branch belonging to Aaron demonstrates that God is closely watching over the DNA strand He gifted you with and He is determined it will rise up and bring forth the fruit He intended it to. No word from His mouth ever returns void but accomplishes the purpose for which He sent it.

He is bringing you forth as part of the company that makes up His servant the branch; the almond branch, budding and awake while others sleep. He is watching over His word, His DNA inheritance within you, to cause it to manifest or perform. He awakens His book of DNA within your earthen vessel; releasing the codons to sound forth and sing the song God composed when He dreamed you up before the foundation of the world.

In modern technology, D.E.W is an abbreviation for 'Directed Energy Weapons'. Wicked men are currently manipulating the weather and waging warfare with these concentrated light and sound weapons as they try to bring about their plan for the

New World Order, but God the Father is also forming His D.E.W. He has been preparing and equipping His directed energy weapons, full of the seven spirits of God, and He intends to unleash them fresh from the womb of the morning and scatter them all over the earth as an assault offensive against the ranks of the enemy. He will use His D.E.W to set the captive free and open prison doors.

Psa 110:3 Your people will offer themselves willingly in the day of Your power, in the beauty of holiness and in holy array out of the womb of the morning; to You [will spring forth] Your young men, who are as the dew.

Chapter 7 ~ Cleansing the Temple with Wine

In the book of Micah, there is a description of breaking through a gate and a group riding through behind their King. Jesus our Bridegroom is the Breaker who goes ahead of us, opening up the way for exercising endtime callings and assignments.

Mic 2:13 The Breaker will go up before them. They will break through, pass in through the gate and go out through it, and their King will pass on before them, the Lord at their head.

When praying, I received a vision which depicted this passage but also connected it to another passage of scripture. I saw the Bridegroom; the Breaker, leading the wine scribes, the Breaker Company out of the gate or portal which He had opened for them to pass through. Then I saw the Lord riding on a donkey and a whole company behind Him, also on donkeys, and they had wineskins under their right arms as they rode. I understood that they were carrying the breaker wine in preparation for pouring it out in the city.

Mat 21:5 Say to the Daughter of Zion [inhabitants of Jerusalem], Behold, your King is coming to you, lowly and riding on a donkey, and on a colt, the foal of a donkey Mat 21:6 Then the disciples went and did as Jesus had directed them. Mat 21:7 They brought the donkey and the colt and laid their coats upon them, and He seated Himself on them.

He is leading forth the wine scribes into the city that was originally 'founded peaceful', Jeru-salem. This name comes from two words, one of which is 'yarah', meaning to flow as water, to point out, to teach and instruct'. The Hebrew word for 'early rain' also means 'teaching'. So the building of Jerusalem is connected to the early rain, the teaching that lays the right foundation. Originally the city of God was built on the right building blocks. It was whole and healthy and functioning well. Now contamination and defilement has taken place and Jerusalem is now called Sodom and Egypt and is no longer a light to the world. So the Breaker is riding in, accompanied by His Breaker Company who will pour out the heavy latter rain of the end-time wine to instruct and restore God's temple and city to His original design and DNA pattern. It is the endtime wine that carries the thunder or voice of God and the heavy latter rain of His eloquent words.

Malachi 3 tells us that the Lord whom we seek is suddenly coming to His temple as a refiner's fire and a fuller's soap. The fuller's soap is used with water usually, but Genesis 49 speaks of a time when Shiloh washes His garment in wine, the blood of grapes. But first the wine must be brought forth. The water within the stone vessels at the wedding in Cana was water of purification, held first within the living stones and cleansing them, before being poured out at the sound of His voice and being transformed into the best wine. Water of purification has a sound, a vibration and a function in preparing the earthen vessel. The effect of His voice is described in Psalm 29 - The God of glory thunders, His voice has been upon the waters stored within the endtime wine scribes. The sound waves have profoundly worked and changed them from the inside out and now the fountain of the deep in the endtime wine cellar is opened for uncleanness for the House of David. And the wine scribes I saw carry it into the city.

Gen 49:11 Binding his foal to the vine, and his ass's colt to the choice vine, he washes his clothing in wine, and his covering in the blood of grapes. Gen 49:12 His eyes shall be dark/brilliant from wine and his teeth white from milk.

Ephesians 5:25, 26 tells us that Christ washes his wife with the water of the Word. In these endtimes, our Bridegroom does not wash His wife with the water of the Word but the wine of the Word. His foal described in Gen 49:11 is His wife, bound in bridal covenant to Him who is the choice vine. Then she is washed in the end-time wine. Notice that the completion of the binding in covenant takes place before the washing of the garment, (and remember the Hebrew word for 'garment' also means 'wife'). The wine of the Word brings to completion the work begun in His Beloved. Interestingly, the gematria for the word 'wine' is 70, as is that of the phrase 'the temple'. Not only that, 70 is also the gematria for the Hebrew letter Ayin, which means eye or fountain'. The fountain of wine is opened for the cleansing of the temple.

The root of the word for 'foal' used in genesis 49:11 means 'awakening'. Song of Song chapter 8 tells us that under the 'apple' tree He awakens us. The word 'apple' in Hebrew means 'breath'. So the foal, His Bride-to-be has been fed with apples of His breath, and all within her that was sleeping has been awakened. The zephyrs of the Seven Spirits have awakened and warmed the sleeping wine within her, imbuing it with the life-bringing breath of God.

However, notice there is also an 'ass's colt'. Who does this depict? The ass's colt is the manchild, also bathed in the blood of grapes. Both the ass and the colt are bound to the Choice Vine which is Jesus, the Bridegroom; one by marriage covenant and the other by bondslave vows. One has come forth from the other. Binding depicts wedding, union, complete alignment and the release of full inheritance, as discussed in the chapter about the Kinsman-Redeemer.

So the bondslave bride and the bondslave manchild are being awakened and prepared for battle by Him who is the choice vine through the washing with wine. They are equally yoked. The word 'bind' means 'to yoke' and they both pull equal weight in bringing forth the purposes of the Kingdom of God. The washing with wine is imperative before full release into endtime ministry can occur.

There is a description in the Book of Revelation of the Breaker riding forth as King of Kings and Lord of Lords, with eyes like a flame of fire. One particular verse is interesting in the context of what we are discussing:

Rev 19:13 He is dressed in a robe dyed by dipping in blood, and the title by which He is called is The Word of God. Rev 19:14 And the troops of heaven, clothed in fine linen, dazzling and clean, followed Him on white horses.

The Greek word translated 'blood' here also means 'the blood or juice of grapes', so this presents an amazing picture of the DNA of the Word wrapped in the end-time wine and riding forth to rule and execute judgment on His enemies, through the sound of the two-edged sword within His mouth.

During the ancient Jewish wedding ceremony, the Bridegroom would remove the Bride's old worn sandals, wash her feet and place a brand new pair of sandals on her

feet. These sandals depicted, without words, the release of inheritance to her as a co-heir. This is why Jesus washed His disciples' feet on the night before He paid the full bridal price. When Peter protested, Jesus said that it needed to take place or Peter would 'have no part' in Him. The feet of the Bride are being washed in the wine imbued with the DNA scroll of what God has prepared for those who love Him. New sandals, full inheritance are being gifted on this day of union. Where does the washing of the feet of the Bride occur? It takes place on the Mount of Olives, where Jesus instructed the disciples to bring the foal and the colt:

Mat 21:1 And when they drew near Jerusalem, and had come to Bethphage, to the Mount of Olives, then Jesus sent two disciples, Mat 21:2 saying to them, Go into the village across from you. And immediately you will find an ass tied, and a colt with her. Untie them and bring them to Me. Mat 21:3 And if anyone says anything to you, you shall say, The Lord has need of them, and immediately He will send them. Mat 21:4 All this was done so that it might be fulfilled which was spoken by the prophet, saying, Mat 21:5 "Tell the daughter of Zion, Behold, your King comes to you, meek, and sitting on an ass, even a colt the foal of an ass."

These verses confirm that the colt is the offspring of the ass and a few verses further on, that garments were placed upon them in preparation for their assignment. They were clothed over on the Mount of Olives, before carrying the presence of the Bridegroom into the city. The washing of the feet of the Bride and the placing of new sandals on her feet is the equivalent of the covering over with garments, the enduing with mantles before walking 'in new shoes', fresh assignments with the Bridegroom.

The Mount of Olives is the place of oil release, of enduing with anointing, the place of the two olive trees giving a ceaseless supply of oil to the two menorahs. They are called 'the sons of oil', God's endtime instruments in the book of Zechariah 4:14 and the two witnesses in the Book of Revelation 11:4.

TURNING THE TABLES

The first thing Jesus did when He entered the city on a donkey was to survey the goings on in the temple. Then He spent the night with Martha and Mary at Bethany on the Mount of Olives, where he was anointed by Mary for His burial, and returned the next day to cleanse the temple of moneychangers and dove-sellers! Those overcomers who are part of the 'head', who possess the mind of Christ and a appointed to rule and reign with Him, must be anointed before they can go forth and partake in the cleansing of the temple.

A 3-fold cord was plaited and used to cleanse the temple, and similarly, there are 3 mediums which will be used to cleanse His Body. In these days, He is going to use fire, light and wine in waves to cleanse His temple and deal with all that has polluted it and distorted its purpose in the earth. The temple of the Holy Spirit was destined to be a house of prayer for all nations, not a den of thieves. So the thieves must be driven out and all impure motives eradicated!

CHANGING GARMENTS

I saw the wine scribes in the city square taking up their wine skins and blowing into them like shofars. They faced the four winds and blew and covered the city with waves of wine-coloured light that blended together and formed a blanket of wine sound, which fell softly covering the whole city, both hiding and shielding and warming. This is the water turned to wine on the 3rd day when all the other wine has run out. I could see movement under the blanket but not what was going on; some sort of rearranging and changing was happening undercover. It looked like when someone changes their clothes with a blanket or towel wrapped round them. There was a hidden change of garment taking place.

So what was the wine 'saying' over the city, I asked? Then I was shown Joshua the High priest in filthy garments, standing before the throne, and the Lord saying, "I always choose Jerusalem,' then rebuking the accuser and calling for a change of garment; rich garments (Zechariah 3). Joshua had just come before the throne as a brand plucked out of the fire and no doubt the heat of the flames had caused all the impurities within to rise to visibility. Satan thought he had ample grounds for accusation. But the brand from the fire has a purpose and a destiny and it is time for CHANGE. Garments suitable for the place he is appointed to stand are brought and he is clothed over; endued with rich garments and a clean turban.

Zec 3:4 And He spoke to those who stood before Him, saying, Take away the filthy garments from him. And He said to [Joshua], Behold, I have caused your iniquity to pass from you, and I will clothe you with rich apparel. Zec 3:5 And I [Zechariah] said, Let them put a clean turban on his head. So they put a clean turban on his head and clothed him with [rich] garments. And the Angel of the Lord stood by.

In the KJV, 'rich garments' is translated as 'change of raiment'. Investiture is happening, a clothing over in glorious garments. The wine is mixed over the city from the wine scribe's wineskins and becomes one unified harmonious sound. Under this blanket of sound, the old filthy garments are removed and rich garments are released and we sink into them. God invests in us authority and a place to stand. No more going out and going into the Throneroom. Now we dwell before His face. He is coming to us as the heavy latter rain, the outpouring of the endtime eloquent wine whose sound around us resounding causes clothing over.

TRADING IN THE OUTER COURT

The sellers of doves got their cages knocked over that day when Jesus took his plaited whip and roared His words of Truth. And the cage doors burst open and those doves soared high into the face of the heavens. That's what they were made for; not being trafficked and traded in the outer court. You see, there are those who want you to trade the image you were created in for another image; one that will put bars around you; one that hems you in, clips your wings. It happens in the Body of Christ, unfortunately, these days. That great temple of living stones isn't joined to the True Head. Blueprints drawn by other builders have wormed their way onto the Message board of the mind of the Body. That's why the Head, the King is coming, full of fiery zeal. There are some messages that need tearing up, taking down.

Doctrines of demons, DNA of Dionysus, would have you worshipping at other altars, forever separated by the bars of idolatry from the throne of God and the light of the seven spirits of God in the Holy Place. Dionysus, god of the counterfeit wine, the wine of Sodom; god of the fleshly pseudo-spiritual experience; that lying spirit who stresses performance and fleshly excellence and harps on drinking from the fountain of his poisonous waters – his days are numbered.

He's the one who cages the doves; those gentle seekers of the Bridegroom whom Song of Songs refers to as 'My love, My dove'. Those who want to soar and follow hard after Him, riding the winds of the Spirit of Truth; they're the ones who have their mantles stolen by the wall-keepers of 'Christian City'. They're the ones stunned by the blow of the words of religious judgment, so they can be easily put back into the cages of religious servitude and trafficked to line the pockets of the dove-sellers.

Son 5:7 The watchmen who go about the city found me. They struck me, they wounded me; the keepers of the walls took my veil and my mantle from me.

Those doves got killed right there. In the outer court, their necks were broken and their blood was spilled for the sins of others. Here's the thing, the blood of doves pacified God, but the Blood of Jesus satisfied God. There's no need for you to lay your life down for another in the outer court. His Blood still speaks for your brother and sister in sin; those who come to satisfy their own sense of guilt at the murderous thoughts they have had concerning your beauty and purity in the Spirit. They want you to pay the price needed for the cloaking of their sin. But the foot of the cross still has space for them to find forgiveness. His Blood still resounds for all who come. There's no need for you to sacrifice yourself; your calling, your destiny, your DNA from the

Book, so another can carry on expressing their gift and doing their thing in the Body without feeling inferior to you. It is written in the volume of the Book concerning you. His thoughts toward you are more than the sand of the sea. You were made to fly in the face of the heavens, communing with your God spirit to spirit. You have an appointed place on the musical score of the magnum opus of Heaven.

I had a vision a short while ago. I saw a giant crocodile flying in the second heaven and it was holding a dove in its mouth. Then, suddenly, its mouth opened and the dove was released to fly away, higher and higher. The demonic entities in the second heaven have been tasked with caging the doves between the teeth of Leviathan, that great twisting serpent/ dragon which the Book of Job describes. He hems you in with stinking flesh coated teeth (Hebrew for 'teeth' means 'teachings') so you can never fly under the unction of the Spirit of Truth within your heart; only getting carried by that carrion perfumed mouth wherever the enemy wants you moved. But now Jesus is overturning the cages of the dove-sellers, driving those vagabonds out of His temple. The powerful sword in His mouth is rendering judgment upon Leviathan, who is holding His doves captive in this day. Suddenly they are released as his power over them is broken and they soar higher and higher in the Spirit.

Isa 27:1 In that day the LORD with his sore and great and strong sword shall punish leviathan the piercing serpent, even leviathan that crooked serpent; and he shall slay the dragon that is in the sea.

RIGHTLY DISCERNING THE BODY

When Jesus cleansed the temple, driving out the moneychangers and the traders of doves, it occurred in the outer court where their tables were set up. The outer court depicts the body, the holy place represents your soul and the holy of holies your spirit. There are some amazing applications concerning the effect which the application of the endtime wine and the communion elements have on our temples, especially in the arena of our physical bodies.

We have focussed so much on the preparing of our souls but our bodies are also destined for full redemption. And it is the moneychangers and the sellers of doves that will be driven out as we partake of the breaking of bread by faith. As the body and blood of the communion meal comes into my temple, the 3-fold DNA whip of God overturns the tables and drives out those destroying and ruining me, be they image-changers or cagers. The power of the Blood of Jesus symbolized by the blood of grapes works powerfully, releasing the sound of His voice in my temple. The law of the Spirit of Life in Christ Jesus sets me free from the law of sin and death. Paul tells us that when we do not rightly discern the body, we become sick or even die. In these days, fresh revelation will be released concerning this passage, which will greatly increase the release of healing through the communion elements.

The moneychangers were men who wanted to change the currency the worshippers carried as a worship offering. They did not consider the image on the coins as acceptable and insisted on an image change, usually at exorbitant exchange rates and the worshippers paid the price. Coins are 'cast' or minted and, according to the image forged upon them, they have authority to transact in the earthly realm. You were originally made in the image of God; that is what your DNA says, but the moneychangers want you to carry and use their prescribed image and 'coin'.

The moneychangers in your outer court (body) represent any foreign DNA which has been taken into your system unknowingly through what you eat or drink. It includes genetically modified (also called GMO) DNA strands from fruit and vegetables, which are sometimes stored in your body because they are not recognized by your digestive system.

What are GMO's exactly? Genetic engineering is the process whereby scientists manipulate an organism's natural state at its most basic level by tinkering with its unique DNA code. This is often by inserting DNA from other organisms. It is thought that at least 70% of processed supermarket foods contain ingredients that have been genetically modified. The food staple that has been corrupted the most is corn (maize), followed closely by soya. When GMO products are removed from the diet, the body is able to begin the process of cleansing the digestive system, healing the damage and restoring its normal functioning according to the blueprint in the God-scripted DNA.

The moneychanger's coinage also includes DNA from aborted foetal tissue which has been used to make some artificial flavourings (you can research on the internet on this horrendous topic). It has also been proved scientifically that women with multiple sexual partners retain the RNA strands from the sperm of each partner inside their bodies for their whole life. No wonder God prescribed purity in the sexual arena with the marriage between one man and one woman. Whatever the source of the moneychanger's 'coin' in your temple, the foreign DNA strands are issuing commands that confuse and interfere with your own body's genetic signalling. The outer court of the temple needs cleansing because it has become a den of thieves - all of whom are intent upon stealing your health and destiny. The last enemy to be conquered is death;

whether it is at work on a spiritual, soul or bodily level. The thief comes to steal, kill and destroy but Jesus came that we might walk in abundant life and health in order to carry out the assignments of the kingdom of Heaven.

Jesus is now coming in this season to overturn the moneychanger's tables and cancel and scatter everything speaking in your outer court, your body, which is not God's original DNA blueprint for your body. This also includes the healing of the memories of all your cells. When a person experiences trauma and pain and extreme stress, the cells in our body keep a memory of that trauma. This is why a person who has had a heart transplant often has memories surfacing which belong to the donor of the heart, often in their dreams.

When Jesus died on the cross, He paid for all trauma and pain to be healed and at salvation and the progressive sanctification that follows, many people experience profound deliverance and healing of emotional pain. However, the record of that trauma locked up in the cell memories of the body still needs to be healed. Sometimes, emotional trauma manifests as physical dis-ease in the body. We are now entering a season when there will be a magnificent wave of physical healing released in the Body of Christ, so that your body can go leaping and dancing, praising God.

DEALING WITH THE SOUND OF DEATH

While the Spirit was helping me to understand these principles, one night I was woken up with Isaiah 36:3. When I looked it up, it described the meeting of 3 people from the king's court with the head of the enemy's army.

Isa 36:2 And the king of Assyria sent the Rabshakeh [the military official] from Lachish [to King Hezekiah at Jerusalem with a great army. And he stood by the canal of the Upper Pool on the highway to the Fuller's Field. Isa 36:3 Then came out to meet him Eliakim son of Hilkiah, who was over the [royal] household, and Shebna the scribe, and Joah son of Asaph, the recording historian.

Eliakim was the governor of the house. In other words, he represents the brain or the mind. The word for scribe means 'to record, tell or speak', so Shebna represents the hearing of the ear in order to speak with your mouth. Joah represents the cell memory; the recorder of the history of your life in written form so it can be read. The enemy king sends a verbal message to the king to basically tell him that he has subdued and killed everyone else he encountered and don't think your God will save you. He speaks decrees of fear and death into the ears of these three emissaries of the king.

I wondered why it was necessary to send both a scribe and a recording historian to listen to the messenger from hell. What the Lord was showing me is that there are two different storehouses of memory in our being. One is connected with normal day to day functioning; record what the King says to your spirit so that your mouth can speak it. The second function of this scribe is to write down or record what the voice of the enemy says so that you can take it to the King of Kings and hear what He has to say about it.

The recording historian however, has a different task. He is writing a book – actually, a series of books! They are the whole long history of your life, every detail of what was said when and by whom. These books or scrolls are not stored in your brain but as a reserve record, a backup copy if you will, tucked away somewhere else as a giant archive. They are a record of the sound waves which have formed and shaped your life from the beginning. And they are stored in cell memory. What happens is that the sound of words of death and hatred; those words intended to invoke terror in you, have an effect within your cells. When trauma has been experienced, there is a scroll of unspoken grief and trauma stored deep in the DNA of your cells.

We see a similar royal archive of records being accessed in the Book of Esther. Between the two banquets which she gave for her enemy and the king, God saw to it that the archive scrolls were brought before the eyes of the king:

Est 6:1 On that night could not the king sleep, and he commanded to bring the book of records of the chronicles; and they were read before the king.

In this case, God allowed memories to surface from deep within the chambers of the palace in order to set in motion the beginning of judgment of the enemy of His people. The exposing of the ambitious plans and designs of the enemy Haman were brought to light and the tables were turned on him. The faithful intercessor at the gate was rewarded and the enemy humiliated. And that evening, after the banquet, he was permanently removed from the king's court and hanged.

Previously the mouth of Haman whispered in the king's ear and orchestrated destructive plans to be unleashed against God's people. But how did he get the king's ear in the first place? The king experienced trauma and betrayal from people in his inner circle whom he had trusted and as a result made a bad judgment call, allowing Haman with his charming words to become his only advisor (Esther 2:21-3:2). Haman had the signet ring of the king and could make laws and sign decrees to further his own purposes to destroy the people of God and raise himself up to rulership. In the same way, the voice of the accuser has been given access to the inner ear of the system in your brain which governs your body and has instituted actions in your body which are destructive and debilitating.

But now, in this season, Jesus is cleansing and healing our temples and exposing the hidden places from which the enemy has been operating. The King of Kings is taking back His temple and driving out the defilers. Health issues which have been battled for decades without any resolution in the saints will now be made clear and the tables overturned on the operating place of the enemy in your outer court.

There is a powerful passage in Zechariah 1 which also illustrates this cleansing and restoration. Zechariah describes four powers or horns which have been working to scatter and cause confusion in the land:

Zec 1:19 And I said to the angel who talked with me, What are these? And he answered me, These are the horns or powers which have scattered Judah, Israel, and Jerusalem. Zec 1:20 Then the Lord showed me four smiths or workmen Zec 1:21 Then said I, What are these [horns and smiths] coming to do? And he said, These are the horns or powers that scattered Judah so that no man lifted up his head. But these smiths or workmen have come to terrorize them and cause them to be panic-stricken, to cast out the horns or powers of the nations who lifted up their horn against the land of Judah to scatter it.

The word for smith also means 'engraver' and this has to do with writing or imprinting a design or message. The engravers are released to terrorize and cast out the powers that have been working destruction. Once again, in this passage the word for 'nations' can also be translated 'foreigners, locusts'. So the engravers are casting out the foreign powers which have been eating like locusts and causing damage and crop failure. Praise God! (We will discuss more about the engravers in Chapter 9). Immediately after this, Zechariah is shown a man with a measuring line. He has been sent with a wonderful purpose:

Zec 2:1 I lifted up my eyes again and looked, and, behold, A man, and a measuring line in his hand! Zec 2:2 And I said, Where are you going? And he said to me, To measure Jerusalem, to see what is its breadth and what is its length.

The word for 'measuring' also means 'a portion, a vestment, a garment'. So the city is being measured for a new garment. She is going to be clothed over!! Once the destructive powers issuing instructions which caused confusion are driven from her, it is time for rich garments. She is the apple of His eye and Zec 2:5 says God is going to be a wall of fire round about her and glory in the midst of her!

Soon after that, Zechariah is shown Joshua, the High Priest, receiving his new garments, once satan has been rebuked by the Lord. The words of death and accusation are silenced by the voice from the throne (this DNA record from satan's library is muted once and for all) and the plans and purposes of God, written in His Book, His DNA scroll, are then sounded forth over Joshua, before being manifested.

You have borne the image of the earthly. Now it is time for you to go forth bearing the image of the Heavenly. The image of the Heavenly involves being clothed over. An image is produced on the outside of the coin and indicates its value and authority to transact in the earthly realm. Joshua the high priest could not stand in his appointed place until he was reclothed. Then he received new authority to function in this place (Zech 3). The garment seen outwardly was part of the investiture into an appointed place of authority and he is clothed over as preparation for receiving a crown of rulership and functioning in the two offices of king and priest.

This of course is a veiled type of the investiture of the Melchizedek priesthood, who rule as kings and priests in the earth with the seven spirits of God equipping them for their kingdom assignments. Before Joshua was just functioning in a priestly role, but after the change in garments and the crowning, he was released to rule as a priestly king. Melchizedek, king of righteousness, was a priest of the Most High.

In Isaiah 49, there is a description of a Bride getting dressed for her wedding. It is the final part of the Bride making herself ready. She clothes herself and puts on her jewels last. Let's look at this passage from a totally new angle:

Isa 49:17 Your sons shall make haste; those destroying you and ruining you shall go out from you. Lift up your eyes all around and see; they all gather and come to you. As I live, says the Lord, you shall surely wear them as an ornament, and bind them on as a bride. For your wastes and your deserted places, and your land of ruins, shall even now be too narrow to dwell in, and they who swallowed you up shall be far away. The sons of your bereavement shall yet say in your ears, The place is too narrow for me; make place for me that I may live.

In Isaiah 49:17, the sons mentioned are your DNA, your seed. Do you remember the children I saw, the codons waking up and presenting themselves in the DNA strand? This passage says that the sons come to meet her and those destroying her flee. Can you see the moneychangers fleeing and the newly awakened and functioning codons releasing their sound? The Bride clothes herself with her sons as an ornament. They are her jewels, the glorious riches of His inheritance gifted her; precious treasure which has been beyond her sight until now. What does putting on your jewels look like when we are considering the awakened DNA codons?

The word for 'ornament' also means 'mouth'. So you are clothed with them as with a 'mouth', a portal to release sound. The Bride is clothed over with all her codons, endued with these children that have come to light. These codons newly awakened and sounding form a new garment, the Melchizedek tent, which wraps around you. This is why you must enlarge the place of your tent (verse 20), because the sleeping codons are awakening and they need space to dwell upright and functioning.

Chapter 8 ~ The Treader of Grapes is Coming Near

One morning in my time with the Lord, I asked Him to show me more about the zephyrs. Immediately I found myself back in the endtime wine cellar and as I looked at the zephyrs being released from the corked bottles, I saw that they carried baskets full of jewels. As they danced on the wine, they tossed jewels down and trod them into the surface of the wine, like one kneads raisins into bread dough. The jewels were different colours and it was given me to understand that they were impartations of the Spirit of the Sovereign Lord, Wisdom and Understanding, Counsel and Might, Knowledge and the Fear of the Lord. The wine was being packed full of nuggets of the seven spirits of God. They were taking that which is part of all of the treasures of wisdom hidden in Christ and imparting it to the wine so that it was enriched 7-fold.

As this happened, I heard the following words, which were describing what was actually being accomplished by this trampling of the jewels into the wine. Once again, as I heard them, I was immediately given the understanding of what they meant:

<u>Imbuing</u> - to fill with a substance or feeling
The endtime wine was being filled to the brim with the substance or impartation of the seven spirits of God. This, in effect, increased the spiritual power held within the wine seven-fold. The word 'seven' in Hebrew also conveys the idea of completion. So 'seven times' actually means 'a double portion'. This is the mantle of Elisha being formed from the mantle of Elijah; the same wine being 'spiced' or permeated with another equal portion of power, in preparation for pouring out.

En-riching – increasing the amount of wealth contained

The imbuing with the jewels by the zephyrs is imparting the riches from God's treasury into a consecrated vessel. He is the God of Riches and Proverbs tells us what Wisdom (Christ Jesus is made unto us wisdom from God) has to say:

Pro 8:18 Riches and honor are with me; enduring wealth and righteousness. Pro 8:19 My fruit is better than gold, yea, than fine gold; and my increase is better than the best silver. Pro 8:20 I walk in the path of righteousness, in the midst of the paths of justice; Pro 8:21 to cause those who love me to inherit wealth, and I will fill up their treasuries.

Inside you is a treasury, a spiritual storehouse and if you seek wisdom daily and love Christ with all your heart, you can ask for the filling up of your treasury. I was shown the process of preparation of the endtime wine, packed full of true riches.

En-hearting - imparting God's heart

The treading in of the jewels into the wine is imparting the heart of God; the desires and longing of His heart for the lost, the hunger He has for intimacy with His Beloved, the compassion He has for the suffering ones. This is very important as faith works through love and our hearts have to be moved with compassion like Jesus was when He gazed upon the crowd following Him. When our hearts move in unity with God's heart and blaze with passion for the things He is passionate about, then the wonder-working power of God is released through our words and prayers.

N-starting - impartation of inheritance (N-heritance)

This new word coined by the Spirit speaks about the starting or enactment of the measured portion of inheritance to the heirs of God. It is one thing to know a piece of land is yours by inheritance; it is quite another to walk its length and breadth and dwell there, enjoying all it has to offer. I was also told that the 'N' stands for the word 'nun', which I know from my studies is a Hebrew letter and also a name. The letter nun represents Perpetuity, Posterity, Heir and Inheritance.

The man named Nun was Joshua's father and the Hebrew name means 'to resprout, to be perpetual', similar to the alternative name for the month of Tishrei, which is Ethanim, meaning 'continuously flowing streams'. In other words, this impartation signifies the initiation of a flow of inheritance that cannot be blocked or dried up. It comes from Him Who is eternal; Whose wealth and resources do not run out.

The word 'nun' is used as a verb only once in the scriptures, in psalm 72:17, where Solomon wishes the name of the king of Israel to 'nun' or continue (propagate).

*Psa 72:17 His name shall endure for ever: his name shall **be continued** as long as the sun: and men shall be blessed in him: all nations shall call him blessed.*

The only way a king's name can continue or propagate is by sons coming forth to carry the family name. Not coincidentally, the ancient pictograph of the Hebrew letter nun looks like a seed or sperm. So the N-heritance is talking about the portion assigned to the sons or seed of God.

Seed brings forth according to the DNA sequence it contains. The sons of God will bring forth in the earth according to the volume of the Book that they have engraved within their hearts. When the words engraved begin to speak or manifest their sound in the sons of God, manifestation in the flesh or the earth results.

However, as I discussed in the previous chapter, foreign DNA can end up in the human body, sowing confusion as to assigned function of the functioning parts. And your own DNA can be damaged. The same is true of the Body of Christ. Some cells or members of the Body are not fitly joined to the Head, as they are receiving instruction from the implanted DNA scrolls of demonic doctrine. This sows utter confusion in the Body and every joint cannot supply. No wonder He is coming as a Refiner's fire and a Fullers' Soap to cleanse His temple. The sound of His voice will reverberate in His Body as He deals with His enemies, the moneychangers and sellers of doves defiling His temple.

Isa 66:6 A roaring sound from the city! A sound from the temple! It is the sound of the Lord rendering recompense to His enemies.

The roar of the Lion of Judah which expresses His passionate jealous love will accomplish the cleansing of His temple. The verse number above is interesting as 666 is gematria for 'the holy crown' and Proverbs 12:4 tells us that a virtuous woman is the crown of her husband. So Isaiah 66:6 is describing the cleansing of the crown or wife of the Lamb, in order to bring holiness to completion.

There is a very interesting verse in Amos concerning the harvesters. It has been preached on in the vein of blessings overtaking the saints but I believe there is a much deeper meaning to this passage;

Amo 9:13 Behold, the days are coming, says the Lord, that the ploughman shall overtake the reaper, and the treader of grapes him who sows the seed; and the mountains shall drop sweet wine and all the hills shall melt

The word 'overtake' is the Hebrew word meaning 'to come near or bring near; euphemistically to lie with a woman; to cause to come up higher'. So we see that the one who ploughs or engraves causes the reaper/ harvester to come near for the purpose of writing upon the ground of their heart. The word indicates that closeness and intimacy is the atmosphere in which this engraving is carried out.

Remember also that in the passage in Matthew where two women are in a field and one is 'taken' and one is left, the word 'taken' also means 'to receive near, to associate with oneself'. I believe this separation and choosing is on the basis of those who have ears to hear. So the plowman will 'come near to' or have intimate conversation with the reapers.

Who is the ploughman? 'Ploughman' in Hebrew means 'to engrave'. He is the One who engraves His word upon our hearts. So the Engraver will come close to and engrave upon the hearts of the reapers the instructions and blueprints for the next season. When Moses and the Israelites came to Mount Sinai, Moses went up the mountain for 40 days to receive the engraved tablets and detailed instruction for the building of the tabernacle. In the same way, the Engraver will write upon our hearts His marriage covenant and give us detailed blueprints to be fulfilled in this season of building the true temple of the Lord. The harvest is going to be brought in and we must be led by the Spirit in all that is done.

Just as God is the initial and ultimate Engraver upon the heart, so too there will be a company of disciples who have grown to mature manhood and declared ready to take over their Father's business of engraving upon the hearts of men.

After the ploughman has passed by and created a furrow in the earth, then the seed is sown. The sower of seed follows the ploughman. This speaks to me of two waves of endtime ministry, much like John the Baptist preparing the way before Jesus follows up. John ploughed the soil of people's hearts and then Jesus, the Seed of God, continued in the same vein, preaching a gospel of repentance and sowed His words in the prepared soil of people's hearts.

NEW WINE FLOWING

The Spirit reminded me of the zephyrs released and dancing in the end time wine vat. So the treaders of grapes, the zephyrs of the seven Spirits of God, will impart to the seed-sowers the measured anointing of the seven spirits set apart for this time, so that they may bring forth the new end-time wine. Remember that after the seed-sowers have encountered the zephyrs, Amos tells us that the mountains will drop sweet wine and the hills will melt. Mountains are those who surround and protect. Hills are obstacles in the journey. So this outpouring of new sweet wine will cause the levelling of the path before those who drink of it. We know from Psalms that the hills only melt at the presence of the Lord, so the new wine flowing forth must be carrying His manifest presence within its folds. As the wine is poured out, it has a profound effect.

Psa 97:5 The hills melted like wax at the presence of the Lord, at the presence of the Lord the whole earth.

Song of Songs also tells us an amazing effect which this best wine kept 'til last has on those who hear its sound:

Son 7:9 And the roof of thy mouth like the best wine for my beloved, that goes down sweetly, causing the lips of those that are asleep to speak.

So the best wine released from the Beloved's mouth awakens those that sleep; the sleeping codons. It awakens the sleeping DNA and causes it to speak or release its sound within!! How important this endtime wine release is! It awakens the sleeping giftings, callings and instructions written in the volume of the Book; those blueprints designed and written especially to create and bring you to completion, for the praise of His glory.

Chapter 9 ~ Bone of My Bone, the Branch

Let's come full circle to the pouring of wine which I mentioned in my Introduction – the Tabernacles outpouring. The reason the wine is poured out of a silver jug onto the altar during this feast is that the first portion of any new bottle of opened wine is always served to the Master of the feast, so that He can check its quality before getting the servants to dish it out to anyone who is thirsty. So we know that this worship offering wine is wine that has not passed the lips of man; it has been set apart for the Lord. The firstfruits belong to Him. After falling on the altar, it is channeled into the silver bowl connected to it. In other words, the silver bowl receives the best wine reserved for the last time, for the prophetic fulfillment of Tabernacles. And do remember that there is a double portion outpouring received into the silver bowl at the altar during Tabernacles - both waters from the pool of Siloam (known to open blind eyes and heal lepers), and 3rd day wine which will cleanse and equip all who are thirsty at the feast.

John 2, where we read the story of the miracle at the wedding at Cana, tells us that the water which was transformed into wine came from 6 stone water pots; normally used for purification purposes by the Jews (washing of hands and feet). So we know that this living-stone pot or vessel has undergone the necessary purification and actually holds within waters which bring cleansing. The wedding at Cana is a prophetic type of the endtime fulfillment of the Feast of Tabernacles, when God's presence as the Master of the Feast in the midst of us is celebrated.

This living stone has made herself ready for her role in the feast of Tabernacles; also called 'the Season of Our Joy'. She has held the living waters of purification from the Eternal Word of God deep within her heart; become fully cleansed and ready to be about her Father's business. The treasure held within her is about to be poured out as a fountain is opened for uncleanness for the house of David. And the first thing Jesus, does is to instruct the bondslaves to fill this stone vessel to the brim; to the point of overflowing!

Joh 2:7 Jesus said to them, Fill the water pitchers with water. So they filled them up to the brim.

Do you remember the zephyrs adding more to the contents of the vat in the endtime wine cellar? They were filling the wine to the brim, making it completely full with seven measures of the Spirit. And here at Cana, we see the same principle being enacted. Before the wine can be poured out of the vessel, the vessel must be completely filled, not just with the firstfruits of the Spirit but with the complete measure that it is possible to contain. Only then is this vessel ready for outpouring at His command. And the transformation occurred in the pouring out. Water went in and wine came out. Within the interior of the vessel, the atmosphere necessary to effect a miracle is present.

This prophetic wedding took place at Cana and of course, no small detail in the Word of God is irrelevant. No location is chosen by chance. It is not by chance that the miraculous outpouring occurred from the stone vessel. And it is significant that this wedding took place in a small village by the name of Cana. This is the place where Jesus first displayed His glory:

Joh 2:11 This beginning of miracles Jesus did in Cana of Galilee, and manifested His glory; and his disciples believed on him.

 The root of the word 'Cana' is 'quaneh', meaning 'a reed, a rod (especially for measuring), bone, branch, calamus'. At the place which comes from the 'bone', the 3ʳᵈ day wine, or the blood of grapes, is created and poured forth, in exactly the same way as the red blood cells come forth from the bone marrow. The body makes about two million red blood cells every second inside the bone marrow. The marrow is inside the bone, just as the wedding is happening inside Cana.

The root of word meaning 'bone, branch, reed' means 'to erect, that is, create; by extension to *procure*, especially by purchase); by implication to *own*, redeem'. The Kinsman-Redeemer purchased us and our field for His possession. So now we are bone of His bone. And from within us, as the Last Eve, there shall come forth the end time wine; the blood of grapes. And as we do, His glory will be manifested.

BRINGING FORTH THE BRANCH

The other meaning for quaneh is 'branch'. The Book of Zechariah speaks of the bringing forth of the branch who will build the true temple of the Lord. After Joshua, the high priest has received his rich garments and a clean turban and told about the places he will be given to walk in before the throne, reference is made to this coming branch as God also mentions a stone with seven eyes:

Zec 3:8 Hear now, O Joshua the high priest, you and your colleagues who [usually] sit before you--for they are men who are a sign or omen [types of what is to come]--for behold, I will bring forth My servant the Branch. Zec 3:9 For behold, upon the stone which I have set before Joshua, upon that one stone are seven eyes or facets [the all-embracing providence of God and the sevenfold radiations of the Spirit of God]. Behold, I will carve upon it its inscription, says the Lord of hosts, and I will remove the iniquity and guilt of this land in a single day.

And then again, once Joshua has been crowned, God announces that this action has completed the bringing forth of the Branch:

Zec 6:11 Then take silver and gold, and make crowns, and set them upon the head of Joshua the son of Josedech, the high priest; Zec 6:12 And speak to him, saying, Thus speaks the LORD of hosts, saying, Behold the man whose name is The BRANCH; and he shall grow up out of his place, and he shall build the temple of the LORD: Zec 6:13 Even he shall build the temple of the LORD; and he shall bear the glory, and shall sit and rule upon his throne; and he shall be a priest upon his throne: and the counsel of peace shall be between them both.

A priest upon a throne, this is not something that occurred in the Aaronic priesthood. So we know that God is referring to a different priesthood; one which functions in both a priestly and a kingly anointing. This describes the Melchizedek priesthood being brought forth. Note it says 'he shall bear the glory'.

On 20th September 2018, which fell during the 10 Days of Awe, I had a dream in which my vision was constantly zooming in and out towards a star in the right shoulder of a constellation which had a raised right arm. On waking, I discovered the constellation was Orion and the particular star was named Betelgeuse. Orion depicts the coming triumphant Prince. Orion was anciently spelt Oarion, from the Hebrew root, which means 'light'. So that Orion means 'coming forth as light'. The name of the star God was highlighting in my dream means 'the coming of the Branch' and it is considered 700 times bigger than our sun! By mid-September to mid-March (best in mid-December), it is visible with the naked eye to virtually every inhabited region of the globe. This is significant as it tells us that every eye will see the coming of the Branch; the triumphant king of glory manifested in His Mechizedek priesthood all over the earth.

The coming branch in the shoulder of the right arm of Orion also speaks of the Lord's strong right arm:

Psa 44:3 For they got not the land [of Canaan] in possession by their own sword, neither did their own arm save them; but Your right hand and Your arm and the light of Your countenance [did it], because You were favourable toward and did delight in them.

This coming Branch Company will operate in the 7 spirits of God, like the stone with 7 eyes, and will carry the glory of God and rule with shalom. They will do mighty exploits and carry His authority (the shoulder where Betelgeuse is situated is the place of authority).

There are two important mentions of Melchizedek which tell us more about this ruling priesthood that is about to be released. The first is in Genesis 14 where Melchizedek meets with Abram and serves him bread and wine:

Gen 14:18 And Melchizedek, king of Salem, brought out bread and wine; and he was the priest of the most high God.

Those who are part of the Melchizedek Priesthood bring forth fresh heavenly bread when there is a famine of the Word of the Lord and they also have access to the endtime wine; the knowledge of the deep things of God – the heavenly things Jesus spoke about.

Joh 3:12 If I have told you earthly things and you do not believe, how shall you believe if I tell you heavenly things?

Hebrews 7 tells us that Jesus was made a high priest after the order of Melchizedek, not on the basis of the Law's requirements but on the basis of an endless life. It is the resurrection life, the zoe life vibrating within Him that qualifies Him for this order. And likewise, those who are reclothed and anointed to operate as both kings and priests will also be brim-full of that same resurrection power.

LET THE BASS NOTES SING

Remember the chapter about God's Magnum Opus and the vision I had of the musical notes pouring out of the woman and finding their places on the musical score? Well, last Sunday, I was singing in tongues and the notes coming out were the deep bass notes of the scale. I knew from my previous studies that God was going to show me something about using the 'base' or foolish things of this world to confound the wise. Base and bass both sound the same and as I studied the scripture where this is mentioned, I had discovered that the Greek word for 'base' is 'agenes'; without genes. Agenes also means 'of unknown descent, and by implication, ignoble'. This word only occurs once in the whole Bible.

1Co 1:28 and God has chosen the base things of the world, and things which are despised, and things which are not, in order to bring to nothing things that are; 1Co 1:29 so that no flesh might glory in His presence.

The Holy Spirit connected this concept to the scripture about Melchizedek being without father or mother:

Heb 7:3 without father, without mother, without descent, having neither beginning of days nor end of life, but made like the Son of God, he remains a priest continually.

Anyway, as I began singing the bass notes, I prayed for the Lord to anchor them in their place on the musical score. And suddenly I saw a vision of the bottom drawer of a chest with 3 drawers being opened and musical notes streaming out and finding their places on the score, where other notes were already placed. I knew that the Melchizedek Priesthood, which has been hidden until they are fully prepared, is now being manifested or brought to light in Heaven's appointed time and very quickly each one will find their place in God's Magnum Opus. They are those well versed in the deep things of God, having been tutored in the shelter of the secret place of His presence. The musical composition has not been complete without them and the orchestra has been waiting for them to be set in place, so that they can strike up the first note and fill the earth with the endtime symphony of sound coming from God' s army, precisely positioned and anchored.

The root of the word 'agenes' means 'to cause to be ("gen" -erate), to become (come into being), arise be assembled'. The Melchizedek Priesthood is involved with causing the army of God to arise and be assembled. Until they emerge into the light, any sound that is released from His people is like the playing of the organ without using the foot pedals, which release the bass notes.

The bottom drawer is a reference to the habit of brides to gather together equipment they will need for married life, even while waiting for the wedding. The Melchizedek Priesthood Company emerges equipped and ready for the plans of God to be brought to completion. From their bellies, the endtime wine pours profusely; the heavy latter rain outpouring of the deep things of God that brings the harvest to completion.

Selah

Further writings and artwork can be found on my website:
https://freshoilreleases.wordpress.com/

You are also welcome to contact me at freshoil@polka.co.za